A Farm Of Our Own

A farm of our own

a spiritual journey running a smallholding

by
Graham R Irwin

CITYSCAPE BOOKS

First published in 1998

British Library Cataloguing in Publication Data

A catalogue record for this book is available from the
British Library

ISBN 0-9533331-0-8

set in Bookman 10 point

Published by CityScape Books
PO Box 16554, London SE1 5ZS
Email: irwin@compuserve.com

Printed and bound in Great Britain
by Biddles Ltd, King's Lynn

To Rosemarie

contents

preface

If someone jogged your arm at the bar and told you he knew a high-tech guy who'd bought himself a small farm, I wouldn't be surprised if your mind went immediately to Richard Briers' 'Good Life' TV series – or even, maybe, to the escape route the fictitious Reginald Perrin took when he opted out of business life and disappeared.

Graham Irwin took that good life option, but not just to get away from it all. A spiritually-minded man, who has that rare approach to life whereby ethics, morals and conscience play a major role, he took off on a ten-year adventure – a life journey he calls it – when he bought a small farm in rural Bedfordshire.

It was in 1997 that Graham approached me with his story of that adventure, that journey of a lifetime, and I became involved in reading and commenting on his work. I was impressed. No, I was more than that – I was uplifted.

Here was a man of great business acumen, with a degree in computer science, taking on nature. But this is not merely a personal tale of a battle with the countryside and its vagaries, or a love for animals, or even his own satisfaction of seeing things grow and happen.

This is a story of people, animals, nature all coming together to bring joy and sadness in sometimes unequal doses and the man living through it to experience a new spiritual plane that set him onto a new path.

Coming to terms with the countryside, with farming, with people, with animals, with the elements, with a new way of life, Graham Irwin found his ten-year journey to be an exciting story he now wishes to share. I have been enthralled by his work and his courage, entranced by his anecdotes, made envious of his achievements.

Each of us has secret hopes and dreams we never get the chance to experience, or maybe just haven't the bravery to tackle. Graham had that courage and, because of it, he found himself. From being a born-and-bred townie from north London, to a 36-year-old part-time farmer and full-time businessman is no mean achievement.

As a youngster, I was given a tongue twister by one of my teachers... 'There are forty thousand feathers on a thrush's throat.' Graham Irwin's tale of country life is no tongue twister, but it is a mind-bender that just may make you think about life, what it means and what it is all about.

Read on and enjoy... I did.

Ken Ashton
Media Consultant

Ken Ashton is an award-winning journalist, a writing tutor, a former mayor of Prestatyn, in north Wales and a townie like Graham Irwin.

author's note

Why would anyone want to read a book about the adventures and experiences of an unknown person? This was a quandary I faced many times in the course of writing this book. It was a question I studiously avoided answering for many months. I just knew that somehow I had to write about my experiences. Encouraged by friends, and driven on by some inner impulse, I just kept going, never quite sure how it was going to finish up. It went against all I had been taught about writing: to know your market before you even put pen to paper. But I trusted there was a reason behind it all and that it would turn out right in the end.

For one thing writing can be a very powerful means of understanding and coming to terms with our innermost thoughts and feelings, as anyone who has ever kept a diary or journal will know. Sometimes the words that come out on the paper can be unexpected, but on reflection turn out to contain greater truths than those we spend ages agonising over.

Most of us seem to embark on different projects throughout our lives not knowing where they will lead. And it is often not until some time after the end of an episode – if at all – that we realise what lessons we have learned and what insights we have gained. My farming experience, as well as writing this book were two such projects for me.

It is not until the last chapter that I have talked about the lessons I have learned as a result of this farming adventure. Although this may give a slightly disjointed feel, it seems to me to be the right place for them, not least because many of these lessons only became apparent long after I left the farm.

So why would anyone want to read about my life? Or even part of my life? The truth is they probably wouldn't! Yet I believe there are many people who would like a 'peek through the keyhole', to see how the other half lives. To share some of another person's experiences; to share their joys, their upsets, their frustrations, their pain, their wonderment of nature. To laugh with them, and at them; to get angry with them, and at them, and for them.

This book is for everyone who has a dream. Whether that dream is to get away from it all, to make a difference in the world, or something a little less dramatic. If it encourages others to follow their dreams then I believe it will have served its purpose. And, if it also entertains, informs, amuses and, perhaps, gives something of an insight into the mysteries and realities of farming life, then even better.

Whatever your dream, I urge you – go for it! Do it now. What have you got to lose? And just think of what you might gain.

Graham Irwin
July 1998

1 A Farm of Our Own

It started on a cold, drizzly October afternoon in 1986. The weather hardly made ideal viewing conditions, but we weren't going to let a little thing like that dampen our enthusiasm.

The moment we saw Home Farm we knew it was just what we'd been looking for all those months. There was a little less than three and a half acres of land. It was less than we had originally hoped for when we started our search but was as much as we could afford without having to live in a caravan. And, much to our surprise, it was only about twenty miles from where we were then living in east Bedfordshire.

Our search had taken us through an area from Essex in the east to Oxfordshire in the west, and from Hertfordshire in the south to the Cambridgeshire fens in the north. To have found somewhere so close to home came as a bit of a surprise.

I must confess to being a born-and-bred townie. I worked as a computer management consultant in London and was under no illusion that I would be able to give up my 'day job' and settle for the 'good life'. But I had always been fond of animals and had a healthy respect for the countryside. And it would be worth the one-and-a-half to two-hour journey to and from work each day – wouldn't it?

My sister had trained at agricultural college and had had several farming jobs before settling down and marrying a Yorkshire farmer. Our parents seemed to be wondering what they had done wrong that both their offspring should end up farming in one way or another.

My partner of three years, Rosemarie, came from a farming background. She had been raised on a family farm in Devon and was used to feeding and looking after livestock. Or so I thought. I might have questioned her experience, however, had I known then of some of her childhood antics. One particular event she admitted to was, at the age of eight, when her father banned her from milking the cows, having caught her trying to milk the sheepdog! What's more, the dog didn't seem to mind!

Rosemarie worked nights as a nurse at the local hospice. She had qualified as a State Enrolled Nurse (SEN) when the qualification meant something, but she felt her qualification and those years of experience were no longer valued. We felt sure her experience with syringes and needles would be particularly useful.

Just what made us want to buy a smallholding away from civilisation, and raise our own produce on a part-time basis I can't recall. It didn't seem to be the fulfilment of a lifelong ambition for either Rosemarie or myself, nor could it have been a desire to quit the 'rat race', but it seemed like a good idea at the time. And, that 'good idea', having surfaced, did not seem to want to go away. On reflection, perhaps it had been a subconscious life's ambition, after all. It certainly was to become our way of life for the next ten years.

When we arrived to view the property we were greeted warmly, and expressed our wish to see the outside first.

The house, often considered the least important part of a farm, stood close to the road and had been built at about the beginning of the century. It was attractive, although not outstanding, the front being of a sandy coloured brickwork with a row or two of red bricks used as a kind of decoration, and with full-sized sash windows.

Eight stables – or loose boxes, to use the technical term – in an L-shaped block formed a picturesque kind of courtyard with the house, in the middle of which were two rowan trees. We pictured what we might do with each of the stables. Goats in one, a house cow peering out of another, one for the dogs, ewes lambing in another, and goodness knows what in the remaining four. Oh, yes. We would need at least one to store the animals' feed, hay, and bedding straw. The corner stable was bigger than the rest, a foaling box designed to hold a mother and her baby. Above the foaling box was a rather half-hearted clock tower which had neither a clock within it nor a weathervane above.

The side garden was dominated by two majestic old walnut trees, one of which came out of the ground almost horizontally before branching upwards, and there was a hole running right inside its trunk. It looked somewhat precarious, but it had obviously weathered a good many winter storms and would, no doubt, survive a few more. We learned later there had been a pond here at one time, which probably accounted for the tree's distorted shape. And, perhaps, gave it a special character.

There were a few flowers and shrubs in the garden, but nothing that really caught the eye – certainly not at that time of year. The grass was obviously just the old pasture. It was very rough and uneven and had not been laid to lawn.

At the back of the stables was an orchard containing more than forty bush apple trees, all in regimented rows as if waiting for the order to advance. What anyone wanted with that number of apple trees we could not imagine. And, as we found out later, they had been planted far too closely together. It turned out there were only four different varieties of apple. But who were we to complain? It was, after all, one ready-made crop. There was also the added bonus of springtime in the orchard: the trees were an absolute picture dressed in their white apple blossom, with the most exquisite scent.

There was a paddock to the side of the house, which was surrounded on three sides by a tall, traditional hedge – mainly hawthorn with the odd blackthorn and bramble. On the other side, nearest the house, was a line of ten or so tall poplar trees. The grass in the paddock was overgrown and full of weeds, and the ground was in a bad way. It had been used for horses and had clearly not been maintained for years, having simply been allowed to 'do its own thing'. But, as the agent would no doubt have said, it had potential.

We couldn't fail to notice the mound in the middle of the paddock. This, we learned later, was where there had once been a spring. When the stables were erected the old farm buildings that were there at the time were demolished and the debris dumped in the paddock. It was intended to be a bank for the horses, so we were informed. However, it was never completed and it looked just like a dump, the bricks and rubble being clearly visible through the thin layer of soil and grass that covered them.

Having inspected the outside, we were ushered into the warmth of the spacious kitchen, where there was a painting of the house commissioned from a local artist friend of the owners. Like most homes in the country, the front door was seldom used, the main entrance being the back door which led through a small lobby into the kitchen.

A tour of the house showed it had been recently decorated. Tastefully, but not with much imagination. The liberal use of a pale green emulsion paint was rather reminiscent of a school or hospital or some government establishment.

Originally just two bedrooms and two downstairs rooms, the house had been extended some years earlier with what was now the kitchen, and a bathroom and a third bedroom upstairs. None of the rooms, with the exception of the kitchen, was especially large, and I tried to envisage a large family packed into the space originally available.

In the lounge was a lovely warm, welcoming open fire, the heart of the house. We sat with a cup of tea watching the flames lick the back of the grate, whilst we learned something of the neighbourhood.

Some while later we left, elated, knowing one day soon we'd be back to stay.

As we drove home, Rosemarie announced, ''Tis a master thing.' Her soft Devonian burr being especially noticeable when she used one of the 'foreign' phrases from her native county.

✧

Five months later, we moved in. Our only animals at the time were two dogs. Cindy, an alert, greedy, black-coated Collie-cross-Labrador had arrived with Rosemarie from Devon, and Kyrie, who was a Bedfordshire born-and-bred Great Dane. Oh, and I mustn't forget the rabbit and guinea pig.

Both the rabbit and guinea pig were male. The rabbit was called George and the guinea pig, Honey. Yes, Honey – a boy! It might have described his colour, but was rather an ignominious name for a chap. They shared a hutch in what was destined to become the goats' stable.

We soon discovered a lad in the village who wanted to 'borrow' a male guinea pig to father a litter. Honey applied for, and was offered, the position and went off for a two-week holiday to find out what he was made of. We were quite excited and I was all ready to make up a sign, 'Guinea Pig at Stud'. Unfortunately, though, Honey was not up to the job. He failed to deliver. Perhaps he had lived too long with George, or maybe it was his name that cramped his style. Whatever it was, there was not going to be a patter of tiny paws from that quarter. And so Honey settled back into his usual routine with George.

Before we got any livestock we were going to have to make the paddock fences stock-proof. A hedge may make a fine windbreak, but any animals would soon find their way through it. We learned later the previous owners had tried their hand at goat-keeping but had given up after protests from their neighbour that it was escaping into the next-door field and eating his corn.

The fencing for the horses was unbelievable. It comprised just a few broken posts that seemed to be held up by barbed wire and baler twine. It wouldn't have kept sheep in, let alone goats, and was dangerous, too. We had kept back some money from when we moved to pay to have the fencing done professionally. When having it done we decided to fence off a small triangular area nearest the house separately, an area we called the 'Tringle'. This was to provide an additional enclosure for when we needed to separate some of the animals. The most appropriate option seemed to be post and rail fencing to separate the Tringle from the main paddock, and half-round posts round the rest of the field. All of it was covered with four foot high stock-proof wire netting. It was rather costly but we thought it worthwhile to have the job done properly.

When we had first started thinking seriously of buying a farm I attended a two-day smallholders' course at a local agricultural college. It was an excellent introduction on how to run a smallholding, the finances of farming, and the types of enterprise we might wish to consider. It was also an ideal opportunity to meet and discuss with other people in a similar position to ourselves. Unfortunately Rosemarie was unable to attend as she couldn't get the time off work, so I went alone. It would have been more enjoyable to have learned together.

There was a surprising cross-section of people attending the course. A couple of wives of City executives were apparently looking for a different way to spend their time – and, the chauvinist in me suggested, their husband's money. There was one retired gentleman who planned to move to Wales and rear rabbits commercially – somehow the tutor didn't seem too impressed with this idea.

One young couple were not very well off but they seemed to be keen and determined to do something to improve their lot, and to participate in the 'good life'. They lived on an urban council estate and had started off by buying three hens, for which they had made a house and run. They kept the chickens in their garden, but had to get rid of them after a neighbour complained of the smell. They had sold them back to the breeder making a loss on the deal. It was a sorry tale and a sad start for them. I have often thought of them since and wondered whether they managed to get started, or if they had given up.

We also started reading up on the subject. One of the smallholder's magazines we had begun taking started life in the mid-seventies as a self-sufficiency magazine. We had collected many back issues and read some rather wacky articles which included, amongst other things, how to make mats out of string and how to make footwear out of discarded tyres. Although they made interesting reading and we did, perhaps, have a somewhat unorthodox lifestyle, we had no intention of taking things quite that far.

We had the privilege of having our own septic tank. As opposed to a cess pit, a septic tank doesn't need to be emptied. It digests the waste and just flows out into the ditch. A year or two after we moved in, the village was connected to mains sewerage, but it didn't get as far as us. It came within about half a mile and stopped there. That was fine by us. The septic tank never gave us any trouble and it was cheaper than mains sewerage. The only problem was, as the septic tank was in the Tringle we had to be careful when we put animals in there to fence off the septic tank in case they should fall through the manhole cover. The idea of one of the animals falling into the sewage was not one we cared to contemplate.

Unfortunately, all but two of the row of poplars had to be taken down as the horses had chewed away the bark and they were beginning to rot and become unsafe. Already one had been blown down in some storms, and the building society had insisted another, which they considered was too close to the house, was going to have to come down. Although poplar doesn't make good firewood – it spits a lot and doesn't give out a lot of heat – it would be another home-grown crop and would save us a bit of money.

Another early job was to clear somewhere for a vegetable garden. There was a suitable area of about forty by eighty feet beside the orchard which had clearly not been cultivated for many a long year. The area was overgrown with grass and weeds to waist height. That part of the land, including the orchard, was undulating, which, we were informed, indicated it was a vestige of medieval strip farming and that it had probably last been ploughed by a horse.

Clearing the land looked a daunting task but we set to, first of all cutting down the grass with a hand scythe. It was hard work but we were keen. With frequent stops for tea we eventually finished the job, and we then burned all the rubbish we had cut down. We had to be very careful the flames didn't spread too quickly, and we were most concerned lest the wind should catch a spark and set light to next door's thatch.

The grass and weeds were still there but now at least they were at ground height. Then we attempted to kill off the weeds with a flame-gun, but it soon became apparent that flame-guns – or our's at least – were not intended for intensive use on such large areas. Reluctantly, we resorted to commercial weedkillers.

Next was the job of digging over the soil. Since Rosemarie was the keen gardener she started the job using a hand fork. In our clay soils for that size of area, however, it would have been back-breaking work. As she soon came to realise. Once the soil had been worked down it would be a different matter. Then it would be perfectly feasible to keep the area in trim with a hand fork, but not to dig over first time round. So after that initial bout of energy the vegetable plot remained untouched for a few months.

It didn't take us long to realise we would not be able to manage all our land with hand-tools alone. Even cutting the grass in the orchard seemed to be a mammoth task. I used to try keeping the grass to a reasonable height – it didn't need to be like a billiard table – with the scythe, but it was tiring work and the job never seemed to get even half-complete. I became rather despondent.

The first thing had to be a tractor. After all, a farm's not a farm without a tractor, or, as a colleague at work suggested, 'Buying a farm is only an excuse to get a tractor anyway.'

So I bought a 1956 'Old Grey Fergie', or to give it its correct name, a Ferguson TEF 20. It was the TE 20, with its revolutionary three-point linkage system, that changed the face of farming for ever. But then I don't want to start getting technical.

The man selling the Fergies had advertised them in a smallholder's magazine. He was a farmer himself and had at least fifty of the machines, together with a variety of Ferguson implements, which filled a couple of barns. Obviously an enthusiast, he said he could get more for the tractors by breaking them for parts, but would much rather see them being put to good use.

But a tractor by itself was not going to be a lot of use. I was also going to need some implements. I was surprised at how many neighbouring farmers who, on seeing I had a tractor, were keen to sell – or in some cases give – me some antiquated piece of kit. For very little outlay I soon accumulated a trailer, a grass mower, a plough, a set of potato ridgers, and two sets of harrows.

The grass mower was an original Ferguson implement, what was sometimes called a 'finger-bar' mower. When I tried to use it for the first time I found it had several missing parts. Not to be defeated I spent many hours creating makeshift replacements. Nuts and bolts and various lengths of chain were used in profusion. Despite this – or perhaps because of it – I was never able to get the mower going properly, and when some of the other parts dropped off I lost patience with it. It spent the rest of its years decorating the orchard. The plough, also an original, was a single-furrow plough intended, as I learned later, for the light fenland soils of Lincolnshire. It was of no earthly use (no pun intended) on our heavy clay land. And the potato ridgers also never got used except to prop open the field gate from time to time. It is often said we learn by our mistakes. This, then, must have been a period of great learning for me.

One of the best places for buying second-hand equipment is the traditional farm sale. For many farmers these are a day out, an excuse for not working for a few hours, a chance to meet old friends, to see how someone else used to farm, or all of these. I went to several sales without buying anything, although I was often tempted to bid for something thinking it might come in handy sometime for something. But, luckily, I always thought better of it, having asked myself whether I really needed the item in question.

At one sale I found a set of flat rollers. This was definitely something I needed for the pasture and they were not easy to come by. I had to have these. There were plenty of ridged – or Cambridge – rolls, but these were not much use for pasture. There were several lots in the sale before them, but eventually the rolls came up. I bid for them and much to my surprise I got them at my first bid. What's more I got them at a reasonable price. I was quite pleased with how well I had done.

Then panic dawned. How was I going to get them home? It was only about two miles, but it would have been a long distance with the tractor. And, in any case, although I had insured the tractor for use on the road, it had no licence plates, no lights, no horn, no tax, and no MOT. I was never quite sure whether this was legal for a vintage tractor, or indeed, whether mine was strictly a vintage tractor. Anyway I wasn't going to chance it.

The rollers came in three sections, an eight-foot roll and two four-footers. I only really wanted the main part but I would have to take them all. Buyers are always advised at farm sales to take the items they have bought as early as possible in case they are stolen, although they're usually given a week to remove them. Not being one to take precipitate action, I went home and considered the matter.

Eventually I hatched a plan. I decided I could hitch them up to the towbar on the back of the company car using a length of chain, and get them home that way.

As I was hitching them up, I received some strange looks from others who were collecting their purchases, presumably for my unconventional and amateurish method of conveyance. But I was too pleased with myself to be concerned with what they might have thought. I took the main section home first. If the smaller rollers were stolen, it wouldn't be the end of the world. I had to take it very slowly, but even then the rolls made the most dreadful noise behind me. Even though there were few passing cars and even fewer houses, it felt as though all eyes were watching me as I drove along. Certainly no one could have failed to hear me coming!

I left the other sections until the weekend. I had noticed before the sale began that one of the rolls had a crack in it but thought no more about it. As I was taking that section home, at perhaps a faster speed than the first, I heard an almighty crunch behind me. I looked in the mirror and saw to my horror that one half of the roller had broken up. There were pieces of cast iron all over the road. My heart sunk to the pit of my stomach. It was going to be impossible to tow home what was left of the roller in that condition. With great difficulty I dragged it off the road and onto the verge, collected up the broken parts and returned home to consider, once again, what to do.

Meanwhile, I fetched the other set back without mishap, taking it a lot slower than before. The broken roller remained at the roadside for a couple more weeks while I continued to consider how I was going to get it home. I passed it each day on my way to work. Was it just my fertile imagination that it seemed to be mocking me?

A friend, Warren, was interested in buying the small set of rollers which was still intact, and he offered to help me get the broken set home when he came to collect his set. Warren was a resourceful man, brought up in the countryside. He had a tool for most jobs, and if he didn't have the appropriate implement he could always improvise. He brought his father-in-law who, he said, liked a 'wheeze', by which I assumed he meant a challenge, and between the three of us we got the broken set inch by inch onto his trailer and home. It was a great relief to get the rolls home – not that they were going to be of any use to me – and I was very grateful for the help. Warren got his roller at a knock-down price in exchange.

When another local farmer friend, David, saw the rolls next time he called, he said, laughing, 'Oh, so it was you! I heard some idiot had bought a set of rolls at the Barn Farm sale and had broken one of them on the road.'

Meanwhile, the vegetable garden was still awaiting our intention. A local farmer friend, John, offered to plough up the plot for us. What a godsend! With his large five-furrow plough on such a small area it took no time at all. Most of the weeds had been killed off by the weedkillers we had used. But the couch grass, or twitch, was best killed off, as John advised us, by 'keeping it on the move', so it would be unable to take root. And the soil needed working down.

This was a job for Fergie and my newly acquired harrows. Not only did the clods of soil need to be broken up, but, because of its undulating nature, the land also needed levelling at the same time. So every day when I got home from the office, I spent a happy and relaxing half-hour or so exercising my newly acquired tractor-driving skills, going round and round in circles harrowing the ground.

In the spring I ploughed up the patch again. By then I had sold the original plough, which for some strange reason was going to be exported to Australia, and had bought a two-furrow plough, which was suitable for our clay soils. So it was a job I could do myself, the first and, as it turned out, only time I got to use the plough. After that it was the 'rounds' again with the harrows.

After we had been in about eighteen months, the opportunity arose to buy some more land when a neighbouring farmer came to sell up part of his holding. The agent's particulars stated he was selling because he was 'intensifying' his enterprise. However, according to local rumour, he was another victim of the recession and the bank had called in his loan.

It was the chance of a lifetime. We would be most unlikely to get another opportunity to buy some more land that actually adjoined ours. The farmer was selling about forty acres, but we could just about afford a piece of a little more than four acres. After much negotiation, firstly as to whether they would be prepared to split the land, and then not surprisingly over the price, we eventually purchased the additional land. Our piece had once been a separate field, but the hedges around it had long since been removed. All forty acres had at one time been part of Home Farm when it was a commercial farm, and it seemed somehow appropriate that some of it was returning. Now we had a 'respectable' seven and a half acres.

Next we had to lay the land to pasture and erect a stock-proof fence. Even though I had the tractor, sowing grass was not a job I felt able to tackle myself. For one thing I didn't have the right implements, and for another I wouldn't have known how to go about it. It always looked easy to see a farm hand operating his tractor, but I soon realised there was more to it than met the eye. You had to know what adjustments to make on each implement and precisely how to set it up to get the job done right. Each task was a combination of skill and experience.

John, who had ploughed up our vegetable garden for us, sowed the grass seed I had purchased. Each sack claimed to be sufficient for two acres, so I bought two sacks. Halfway round John ran out of grass seed.

'But I bought enough for four acres,' I moaned.

'Ah, you need at least twice what they say in the instructions,' John informed me.

Muttering, and realising this was another opportunity to learn what the books never tell you, we visited a local farm merchant to get another couple of sacks of grass seed. That finished I went over the field with the rolls.

We managed to obtain a grant for a hedge along our border and for 150 oak and hazel trees to create a small copse. The county council would provide all the plants if we supplied the labour. It seemed like a good deal. A council adviser came and drew up a plan, suggesting a traditional hedge comprising mainly hawthorn, or quickthorn, with a smattering of blackthorn, buckthorn, dogwood and guelder rose.

What a winter we had in 1988/89. Each day over the Christmas and the New Year break we spent hours setting more than 400 hedging plants, as well as the

150 trees. As we trudged back and forth our wellies became caked in the thick clay. We soon gave up trying to remove the mud from our wellies every two minutes and simply decided to make the best of it. It was like walking with boots of lead. Boy, was I glad to get back to the office after the break!

That done we had to make the field stock-proof. There were several options, including half-round posts and stock fencing as we had used in the paddock. In the end we decided on electric fencing as our best option. It was cheaper than most of the alternatives, likely to be more effective, and was easy enough to erect for me to be able to tackle it myself.

A local farmer was the dealer for the electric fencing. It was perhaps the best advertisement of all in that he used the fencing himself. He had been trained by the New Zealanders, who had introduced this type of fencing to the UK, in how to install and erect it. I received a potted version, enough to get me going. After a good many attempts I managed quite a passable job at tying the insulators, through which the electric fencing would run, onto the posts. It was no mean feat tying knots in the stiff, high-tensile wire, but it gave me a great sense of satisfaction knowing I had tied them correctly. Once the posts were up and the insulators tied on, it then took over a mile of wire running four times round the field. Next I had to install the fencer unit, which provided electric pulses at 5,000 volts, in one of the stables, and then run cables out through the orchard to the back field. That complete, we finally had our stock-proof field.

It looked as though our new hedge was going to be something of a disaster. No sooner had we planted it than the rabbits and hares from all over Bedfordshire

– or so it seemed – came calling, obviously considering this a veritable banquet. With no grass or crops on either side, the hedge must have stood out like a neon sign saying, 'Eat me!' In no time at all the plants were less than half their original size. And some were left no more than a couple of inches high. After all that hard work, to say we were depressed would be something of an understatement. I was close to despair. The council would replace any plants that failed to survive the first year, but they were unable to offer any advice or practical help. We had been given tree guards for the oak and hazel trees, but it would have been impractical to have guards for over four hundred hedging plants.

We asked one local farmer if there was anything rabbits didn't eat. He looked pensive for a while before suggesting, 'Stones?'

Things seemed to go from bad to worse. After such a bad start we then had several years of drought when nothing seemed to grow very much. Added to which the neighbouring farmer, not being able to see the by now minuscule hedging plants and eager to cultivate every last inch of his field, ran over several of the plants with his tractor. The hedge was a very sorry sight for several years, and we often wondered whether it would survive at all.

We had been advised to keep the new plants free from weeds to stop them being choked and help them grow. It was not an easy task. In fact it was downright tedious and tiring. After a while of hand weeding we tried using a brush cutter, only to find we added to our woes by occasionally lopping off the top of another hawthorn plant. As if the rabbits and the weather weren't enough we started to sabotage our own work!

Luckily for us, though, hawthorn is a very resilient plant. Despite all the efforts of man and nature, we lost only a handful of plants and, although it had a poor start, the hedge did begin to grow. Slowly.

Only after about five years was it at all obvious there was a hedge there at all. I might even be tempted to suggest it started to thrive.

After a couple of years I had become pretty confident at knocking together the odd small farm construction. Having built a couple of poultry houses and a field shelter for the sheep my next project was to make a barn in the back field. It was only going to be a small one by commercial standards, just twelve feet by twenty-four, but for me it would be a major undertaking. And luckily I was able to start it before the planning regulations were changed so I didn't need to submit any plans to the local authority.

First, I needed six poles – either telegraph poles or electricity poles would do – and six holes in which to 'plant' them. Making the holes, each four feet deep, was the easy part using a specially extended auger. Our mate John had found a supply of electricity poles. The tricky part was going to be getting them upright into the holes. I couldn't imagine how we were going to get them vertical and pondered the problem for some while. One day when I was at work David, another neighbouring farmer, called round and whilst they chatted Rosemarie mentioned our predicament. I came home in the evening to find one of the poles upright in its hole.

'What? Er... How?' I spluttered.

'Oh, it was quite easy, really,' she teased.

'But...'

Rosemarie let me stew for a while, confused, bewildered, in awe. She eventually let on that David had lifted one end of the pole, 'walked' his hands down the pole until it plopped into its hole. I didn't know what to say. I was flabbergasted. They were so heavy I could barely lift one end a foot off the ground. But the evidence was irrefutable, it could obviously be done.

The rest of the poles didn't find their ways into their holes quite so easily, but with the use of a scaffolding tower and ropes and the help of friends we eventually had six poles upright in each of the six holes. They were promptly cemented into place as if somehow they might otherwise escape.

The next part was to make three roof trusses, for which the local demolition merchant supplied the timber. The barn's design was based on a plan published in one of the magazines we subscribed to. It had an unusual feature in that all the timber was bolted together rather than being fitted together using traditional joints. It may have been a little unconventional but it made the barn somewhat easier to construct. The roof itself comprised corrugated iron sheets nailed to timber crosspieces, which in turn were bolted to the trusses.

My calculations told me it should take about five hundred bales of hay or straw. This was more than we would need for the animals over the winter and so I decided to have one half of the barn for the hay and straw, and to keep the other half open so we could use it as a shelter for the goats, sheep and cows.

Finally, then, here stood a tribute to our hard work and the help and assistance of our friends and supporters.

2 Village Gossip

The farm was about a mile from the village, not that there was much to the village itself. The entire parish boasted only about 250 houses, and these were scattered over a wide area. The parish consisted of the village itself, including several 'Ends,' and a couple of hamlets. There were no shops, although there was a post office and a pottery, as well as the parish church and a chapel. And sadly the pottery closed before long. There was also a primary school, but the older children had to travel to one of the nearby towns for their schooling. Somewhat surprisingly for a rural area there was a fairly regular, if none too reliable, bus service, with three or four buses a day running between the two main towns – and passing through the village.

We learned there had been a blacksmith in the village several years earlier, but his business had gone the way of the vast majority of village blacksmiths. The only blacksmiths we ever saw, other than those at rural craft fairs, were the farriers who travelled round with their mobile smithy in the back of a van. Not quite the traditional picture of the blacksmith, but practical and convenient. The old village blacksmith had been noted for many miles around, and, so the story went, had given the postman his bearings on foggy days when walking across the fields from one village to the next, the sound of his hammer on the anvil carrying to the next village. However, the postman travelled by van these days.

The area was mainly arable farming, which meant the fields tended to be large and without hedges or gates. Coming from Devon as she did, Rosemarie always contended it was not real farming, as there was no livestock. True farming, she believed, was mixed farming – livestock and crops.

The village was still largely unspoilt by over development and commuters. As a result it still retained a number of characters who had been born and bred in the area. Several of them, it seemed, were destined to become part of our 'support group'.

Our nearest neighbours were two sisters, who, we guessed, were somewhere in their sixties. Connie and Maud had been born and raised in the small, partly-thatched, cottage they still inhabited.

We were told the sisters came from a family of twenty-one brothers and sisters, though we suspected the number increased with each telling, and it was not something we liked to ask about. As local rumour had it their mother had produced one child every year, except one when she had a bike instead. No, we never understood the logic of that either!

Their cottage was very small and we could not imagine how such a large family would have fitted in it, let alone lived there. Neither was it in a good state of repair. It needed rewiring, a new thatch and some structural repairs.

Maud had never learned to read and write and was considered by some in the village not to be 'all there'. But we never doubted she was quite astute and even on occasions quite artful. She smoked like a trooper. We could always tell when Maud had been round by the smell of stale cigarette smoke which seemed to cling to everything she came into contact with.

In the summer she was often to be seen in their garden sporting a pair of colourful Bermuda shorts, which, despite her age, were rather becoming. She also had a penchant for keeping the lawn well shaved, often cutting it several times a week till it was almost bald. Maud seemed to be pretty fit for her age and frequently rode her bicycle the mile or so into the village, either to visit another sister or tend the family grave in the churchyard.

Connie was divorced and had moved back with Maud in order to look after her. Whether Maud really needed looking after or simply didn't like the idea of living alone we were never sure. However, the arrangement seemed to suit them both. Like many siblings they appeared to get on well enough together with just the occasional sisterly disagreement. Grey-haired, good natured, and chatty – though never one for idle gossip – Connie was the more outgoing of the two, usually taking the bus into town every day. Connie suffered from one or two ailments, about which we didn't like to enquire too closely. When she twisted her ankle one year, she had Maud push her around in an old bath chair, sometimes even up to the village.

We worked out a kind of bartering system with Connie and Maud. We gave them apples, milk, eggs and other produce, and I would mend Maud's regular cycle tyre punctures. In return we would get leftovers for the animals, rock buns, cooked pies and preserves, and sticks of rock when they returned from their holidays.

On one occasion Maud brought round a couple of sacks of firewood. It seems she had seen Rosemarie returning from a walk with the dogs, dragging a branch of a tree for firewood a few days earlier. She had been up to the churchyard to tend a relative's grave and had brought back the firewood in her wheelbarrow. Bless her, the churchyard was almost a mile's walk.

Next to the sisters was George's cottage. Not actually his, but a tied cottage that went with the job from which he had retired some years earlier. He had worked on our farm when it had been a commercial enterprise, driving and maintaining the steam engines. He told us a lot of stories about how things used to be on our farm in days gone by. Sadly, though, because of his tendency to mumble we only ever understood a fraction of what he told us. And asking him to repeat everything became rather time-consuming. He explained he used to get his water from a spring in our paddock until about 1936 when mains water was laid on – and even then it was only to a standpipe.

Unfortunately, poor old George often used to become rather confused. We would sometimes find him wandering down the road in his pyjamas at odd times at night. Occasionally, he called round late at night with all his cutlery in a pillowcase, asking us to look after it for him as he had a burglar in the house. We would walk home with him and show him everything was okay, after which he seemed to settle down for the night.

His trousers were covered with cigarette burns and his kitchen table littered with items of stale food, bottles of sour milk, and overflowing ashtrays. That he never set fire to himself or the house was a wonder to both of us.

He always had a biscuit for the dogs when we went past on their walkies. It seemed to be a ploy on his part to ensure we would stop to talk. Unfortunately it always made walking the dogs a rather long and drawn out process, and we didn't always have time for a chat. Sometimes we would try to creep past in the hope we wouldn't be noticed, usually without success.

George told us one time that his son was a guest of Her Majesty. We thought at first he meant he worked at Buckingham Palace or something of that kind, but he later confided he was 'inside' – for what we thought it better not to ask.

Sadly George died during our first winter. In an obituary in the parish magazine we learned of a different side of him in that he had served in the Army in India for seven years, and had been a founding member of the village OAP's club.

Next to George was the pub. Despite its proximity the pub didn't figure very largely in our lives. It seemed we incurred the displeasure of the landlord early on by refusing to rent out our paddock to his daughter for her horse on the apparently 'unreasonable' grounds that we were going to use it ourselves! After that there were a couple of unpleasant exchanges: the first when he complained a bonfire of ours would upset his customers; another when we complained his dog was being allowed to wander down the road without supervision. Although it was difficult we did our best to pretend the pub didn't exist.

Further up the road lived Dorothy, George's landlady and a cousin of Connie and Maud's. Dorothy was a widow who, as we learned after the event, celebrated her eightieth birthday not long after we moved in. She and her husband used to own Home Farm when it had been a commercial farm, and she had moved out after his death. Amongst other things, they had apparently grown chrysanthemums and gladioli in the area that was now the paddock. Dorothy had another farm now with a tiny and rather ramshackle-looking cottage.

She was one of those people who always seems to want things to be different from the way they are. It was evident she missed her late husband, as she often mentioned him in conversation. And it was obvious she wanted company, but she seemed to have become rather bitter. Sad to say, conversations with Dorothy were very tiring as they usually involved her moans about life in general or various people in the village. When Rosemarie started receiving irate phone calls demanding a visit if she hadn't been up for a couple of days we decided to avoid visiting her.

Although she lived only about 30 yards from the postbox, whenever she had a letter to post Dorothy would ring Maud to collect and post it for her. It seemed a strange arrangement. Even more surprising to us was that Maud always seemed happy to oblige.

As well as her farm she also ran a petrol pump. It was an old-fashioned type that had to be operated by hand, and must have been one of the last of its kind in daily use in the country. For several years Dorothy ran this pump, despite being the victim of frequent night time thefts. But she was not getting any younger and was unable to compete with general petrol prices. After each theft the police would attempt to persuade her to give up selling petrol, but with no success. The final straw came when she returned one night from an OAP's shindig to be confronted by an intruder in her bedroom. Reluctantly she gave up selling petrol, although the pump remained, a memorial to her stamina.

The village postmistress was a friendly and chatty lady who went by the name of Paula – Post Office Paula we used to call her. As a member of the parish council, as well as the proprietor of the only 'shop' in the village, she knew a lot of what went on in the area.

When we first moved to the area Paula and her family seemed to suffer from more than their fair share of ailments. Rosemarie was always treated to the latest instalment whenever she went in, and always found it difficult to get away. If it wasn't Paula's hysterectomy, her sinuses or her dental problems, it was her husband's stomach, their Christmas trials or her granddaughter's sickness. Whether being a nurse and having enough of medical ailments at work or what I was not sure, but after a few visits Rosemarie decided to use the Post Office in the next village.

John was another villager who seemed to know most of what went on in the district. He called to introduce himself one day a few weeks after we had moved in.

He stood a full six feet tall, his black Labrador dog, Pip, by his side. At a guess he was probably in his late forties. His trousers and work shirt, whilst still serviceable, had certainly seen better days. He spoke with a soft but noticeable Bedfordshire accent, and had the local habit of referring to a male of whatever age as 'the old boy.' This phrase confused us no end for many months, especially when a boy or baby would be called 'the little old boy!'

How John made a living was a mystery to us. Indeed, he was something of an enigma in many ways. He described himself as a farmer, although he owned just ten acres of land and rented another fifteen. And we all knew twenty-five acres was nowhere near enough from which to earn a living. He also kept more than fifty hives of bees throughout the locality and sold several hundred pounds of honey each year through various outlets.

John also enjoyed woodworking and sold several of his creations, which included wheelbarrows, wine racks, seats, and even a garden bench on wheels. He even erected a set of stables for one of our neighbours, but it was not one of his more successful works as it lost most of its roof one night in a particularly strong gale. Still, none of his work seemed to add up to enough on which to keep a family. His most ambitious project was the restoration of an old horse cart, something that would, no doubt, take him several years – if he ever finished it at all.

He had a cheerful disposition and was always ready to stop for a gossip or lend a hand. But he had the most infuriating habit of talking in riddles. He seemed to find it difficult to give a straightforward answer to a direct question. It was as though he found it difficult to commit himself, or perhaps he liked to think he knew something you didn't. On one occasion John was one of those interviewed on the local radio for a programme about the village. He was asked about his beekeeping activities, and had the interviewer stumped when asked what he did when he got stung. John simply replied, 'I just say, "Ouch!"'

John helped me find supplies of apples one year for cider making and was naturally enough keen to sample the results when it was ready. He popped round one day when I was at work and Rosemarie poured him a pint. He insisted on a pint, not a half. It was deceptive in its strength and he drank it back rather quickly.

'Careful! It's strong stuff, John,' Rosemarie protested.

'Oh, it's only cordial,' he replied, dismissively.

When it came for him to go, he got up and obviously felt a little light headed. 'Mmm, it was quite strong,' he agreed, his eyes slightly glazed.

Rosemarie offered to drive his van home for him, but he declined the offer. As he reversed his van and trailer out of the drive and almost into the ditch opposite, she wondered whether she shouldn't have insisted.

John sold us a load of straw one year which we had to collect from off the field. We arrived to find he had almost sold the straw to someone else, but that's another story. We loaded up the trailer with forty bales and Rosemarie perched herself on top, from where, she said, she would have a good view of the neighbours' gardens. We were just about to move off when John said, mischievously, 'The last chap had that trailer loaded it with timber and had his missus perched on top. But the tipper mechanism broke and all the wood and his wife landed up on the road.'

'Thanks, John,' Rosemarie replied, somewhat disquieted.

He assured us the tip-up hitch had been fixed, and pointed to a length of rope wrapped rather haphazardly round the bottom. Rosemarie didn't seem convinced. But, as we headed home, she was true to her promise of looking to see what people had in their gardens. That is until she nearly got knocked off her perch by an overhanging branch. And just to add to her embarrassment she looked behind to find John, who was following behind us in his van, laughing heartily.

We often used to see a little green van, the driver of which always waved as he drove past our house. It was some months before we found out who he was. Clive was another local farmer, who rented the field directly opposite our house and grew a variety of crops. One year he had four acres of Brussels sprouts. That winter he was out every day whatever the weather handpicking his sprouts. It must have been very cold, tiring, and backbreaking work – and for such little return. And some days he was there from seven in the morning till four in the evening.

Another year, on another rented field, he lost all but a handful of plants in a two-acre crop of cabbages. The crop that seemed to give him the least amount of problems was corn, and in later years he seemed to favour this.

It was no great surprise to find he got himself another job, as a lorry driver, and kept his farming as a part-time enterprise.

Only once – in our first year – did we manage to get away for a holiday together. We left our little farm in the care of a friend, Sheila, who, despite her lack of experience, was very keen to animal-sit for us. At the time we had just a few goats – only two of whom were milking – half a dozen hens, two dogs and two cats, so we thought it would be a piece of cake. We agreed to swap our milking goats with two non-milkers from a friend, Mad Maureen. She had so many goats, dogs and other animals, and we never knew what she did with any of them, but she was a friendly and helpful soul. When the two non-milkers arrived, Sheila's face was a picture of stunned horror, and she looked as though she considered going home there and then. One was the most enormous goat I have ever seen. Even I had difficulty holding her – and poor Sheila was only five feet two!

It was hardly a very restful holiday. We would phone every evening to check that everything was alright, but it didn't stop us worrying in between phone calls. When we returned, Sheila informed us that for some unknown reason the goat kids weren't eating their hay. We looked in to their stable to find their hay net filled with straw! It had never occurred to us that someone might get hay and straw confused. And our hens stopped laying for a few weeks just after that holiday, for whatever reason we never discovered.

We also noticed the septic tank was rather smelly. It often had a certain – er... – aroma, but this was somewhat more noticeable and more prolonged. On investigation we discovered Sheila had been liberally dosing the loos with bleach, which had destroyed the bacteria in the septic tank. Our best option was to have the tank emptied and allow the bacteria to regenerate naturally. A process that would probably take two or three months.

Our experience convinced us, if we needed any persuasion, that having someone look after the farm whilst we went away was not worth the worry and aggravation. Although we managed to get away separately for the odd week or extended weekend, we never took another holiday away together.

Maureen was an unusual lady. Somewhat overweight, she seemed to live almost entirely on fizzy drinks, and she smoked heavily. She kept a number of animals, including goats, sheep, ducks, geese and dogs, on a very small area of land – just an extended back garden. Though it was not our place to judge, her stock management seemed to leave a lot to be desired, and all the animals seemed to be kept in rather cramped and not very hygienic conditions. She had a generous nature, but seemed to be rather lazy when it came to caring for the animals. Several times she had to call out the vet for ailments that could, we believed, have been prevented by good management.

Maureen and her husband later rented a two-acre field which they had to grass seed and fence, and on which they erected some home-made housing for some of their goats and sheep. One morning they came out to find the part-complete housing had been blown across the road. It didn't take a genius to recognise it was going to need further strengthening before it was complete. The housing was eventually completed, but not for long. A few weeks later it was burned to the ground. Maureen was distraught, particularly as several animals were killed in the blaze. I find it difficult even now, after all this time, to contemplate what happened, and we never did discover what caused the fire.

Several months after having a new baby, one young couple we knew decided to spread a field with slurry from their cesspit. When he had finished, the farmer looked back at his handiwork to see the field littered with nappy liners. A little too late he found they had not decomposed!

We had bought our straw and much of our hay from Jack, another local farmer. He and his Jack Russell bitch, Suzie, became regular visitors. Suzie would entertain us with her trick of 'brick wrestling'. She would wrap her paws round half a brick – there were always a few lying around the yard – and drag it backwards whilst growling at it. With our Great Dane, Kyrie, and Labrador cross, Cindy, we were not used to small dogs. But we soon became very fond of Sue who, when she was not chewing bricks, was very friendly and affectionate.

We became so fond of her that when one year Jack announced that Sue was having a litter Rosemarie got me two JR puppies for Christmas. And, as if Jack Russells are not small enough, I chose the two smallest pups in the litter. Two black and white bitches whom we named Lucy and Poppy – and who we referred to collectively as the 'weenies'.

It was a mistake having two JR bitches from the same litter, as we were soon to discover. They were never close bosom buddies. But the first time they had a real ding-dong of a fight was rather frightening, not knowing how to handle it. I didn't dare get my hands in the way to pull them apart, so I carefully lifted them, still attached to each other by their teeth, on the toe of one of my wellies, and deposited them outside in the snow. It didn't have any effect. They continued to fight, growling and biting each other with serious intent. The snow was spotted with red, but still they continued to fight. Eventually they seemed to tire of the battle and were sent to their stable in disgrace looking daggers at each other.

Lucy always seemed to come off the worse for their skirmishes, as her jaws didn't quite fit together. This meant that, whilst Poppy's bites made their mark, drawing blood and often leaving permanent scars, Lucy's bites left little, if any, mark on her sister.

Despite their dislike of each other, separately Lucy and Poppy were very affectionate towards us both. And, as I was to discover somewhat later, Lucy was as happy living in town as in the country.

3 Goats

'You don't suppose we spoil the animals, do you?' I called to Rosemarie as she worked in the garden. I was cutting off the remaining wasted autumn blackberries with the secateurs as an evening treat for the goats.

For some reason the question went unanswered. Oh well, I guess it was only a rhetorical question after all. It was pretty obvious. Why else would I be picking blackberries for the goats? But then our animals were not run-of-the-mill farm animals.

The goats were our first livestock. It had been our intention to obtain a few goats to produce enough milk for ourselves with some excess to sell. With this in mind, our first goat was hardly the ideal choice – a yearling, from whom we would have to wait at least a year before we got any milk! So keen were we to get a goat that this oversight seemed to escape us at the time.

Sophie was a white crossbred goat. Very pretty with long dangling ears and a tiny pink nose. But, as we were soon to find out, she was also very scatty and had a manic bleat which was more like a screech that would not have been out of place in a Hitchcock horror film. We got her home and into the stable we had prepared for her and Sophie seemed to be sulking. She wouldn't eat any of the goat mixture we offered her, or any greenery. And then she started running round in circles jumping up at each wall in turn and bleating dementedly. As newcomers to goat-keeping we were frantic with worry.

'What are we going to do?' cried Rosemarie. 'I can't stand all this noise for long.'

'She probably just needs time to settle down,' I suggested helpfully.

'We'll have to do something soon or we'll have the neighbours complaining.'

The farmer from whom we had brought Sophie, Mr Jones, suggested that, since goats were herd animals, she probably wanted company. No, it wasn't a ploy on his part to sell us another goat! At first he said he had no more to sell.

Meanwhile, we borrowed a goat from Maureen. Kiwi was a distinguished-looking, brown Anglo Nubian – the type with a Roman nose and long floppy ears. She was very calm and good natured, and she should have been a calming influence on Sophie. But not much.

Mr Jones eventually agreed to sell us Lin, a heavily in-kid British Alpine – an attractive breed with a black coat and white markings. We collected and brought her home just six days after Sophie, though it seemed much longer.

Lin was a goat of more mature years with an impassive nature, who seemed to take everything in her stride. It was with some difficulty we got Lin into my rather inappropriate hatchback. On the way home the mirth of drivers behind as well as several passersby made us realise poor old Lin's swollen private parts were clearly visible to all and sundry through the back window. Not that she seemed to care.

Getting Lin out of the car when we arrived home promised to be tricky. It had taken two men to lift her into the car, and there was only Rosemarie and me to get her out. However, when I put a bale of straw on the ground to lessen the height she just stepped implacably down onto the bale and then onto terra firma.

Lin kidded at Easter, much to my delight as I was at home to witness the first births on our little farm. Not, it has to be said, that I was of much help. All that blood and placenta! It was a lovely warm sunny day, which was ideal as they could all enjoy the outdoors air. I helped Rosemarie to dry off the kids – two males and a female – and we made sure they knew where to find their milk supply. Rosemarie impressed upon me several times the importance of the first suckle for newborns as the milk is mainly colostrum, which contains natural antibodies from the mother. Ideally they should have their first feed within a couple of hours of their birth.

A few hours after Lin had given birth we saw a couple of boys straining over the gate trying to catch a glimpse of our new arrivals. We proudly asked if they wanted to come in to see them.

'Oh, yes please,' they chorused eagerly. They were almost as excited as we were and wanted to know what breed they were, how long they'd been born, what other animals we had, and would it be all right to come back at the weekend to take some photographs for a school project? We answered all their questions easily and readily as though it were an everyday occurrence for us.

Now that Lin had kidded, we would have some milk. She was not a heavy milker, giving between four and six pints a day, but this was more than enough for ourselves, with some left over to sell. In order to get the milk we had to separate Lin from her kids, keeping them in a separate stable, and hand rearing Rosy and the 'Billy Boys' on dried milk.

We fed them from a wine bottle fitted with a lamb's teat. But they were very rough, frequently knocking the bottle from our hand and fighting over the bottle so we were never sure if they'd each had their fair share. After about six months the kids were so rough we just gave them their milk in a washing-up bowl and left them to it. I've never seen milk disappear so fast!

We planned to keep the female, whom we named Rosy. And we faced a stark choice with the Billy Boys. We were not in the business of keeping them just for pets, and indeed no-one seems to want male goats for pets anyway. So we had two options. We could kill them at birth, an option that took less than a moment to reject. The other option was to give them a few months of good life and have them for meat. Looking after these young creatures and then having them killed did not greatly appeal, but if we were going to eat meat at all it seemed better that we knew the animals had been looked after and had a good life and a quick and humane end. Even if we didn't eat meat there would still have been a difficult decision to be made as to what to do with any male offspring.

The goats spent the nights in the stable and went out into the paddock during the day, unless it was actually raining or frosty, or if there was snow on the ground. Even if it was dull and overcast they went out. Sophie, in particular, called – or rather, bawled – to be put out every morning. But they would soon call to go back inside if it started to rain. Their thin coats were not designed to withstand the rain or cold.

I bought a small field shelter for them for when it did rain, to save us the task of bringing them in every time. It is something I would have made myself in later years. At the first sign of rain we would see Lin sauntering over to the field shelter for its protection. The others would wait until they were more certain it was raining and would then make a mad gallop towards the shelter. But Lin was invariably the first there – and the last to leave it once the rain had stopped. The image of her black and white face peering out of the shelter is still quite vivid.

The stables were not ideal for the goats, but with some minor conversion they proved acceptable. The hay racks, bucket holders, and mangers, having been set at horse height, all needed lowering, of course. We kept three or four goats in one stable. When, a little while later, we had six or seven goats and had to split them between two stables, we found it was too much work. And three or four goats were sufficient for our needs anyway.

There was always a scrum at feeding time. They needed two mangers and two hay racks, as four goats had great difficulty in sharing just one. With the two mangers they seemed to spend much of their time running from one to the other, pushing each other out of the way. But if they wanted to spend their time this way, then that was up to them. It did mean, though, that the goats ate whatever they could, and that we were unable to vary the quantity of feed for an individual goat. But then we weren't that scientific in our feeding anyway. If we did need to give special rations to one of them, then we could feed her outside the stable.

And then with one hay rack they all fought for the hay and much of it fell to the ground from where it would not be picked up. Contrary to popular belief goats do not eat just anything. They will nibble at almost anything, but they are, in fact, very fussy eaters. And they wasted a lot of hay. Learning that all goat keepers had the same problem was not much of a consolation.

In order to milk them we took the milking goats out of the stable one at a time and fed them their ration of goat mix, whilst we pulled on the other end. Occasionally one of the non-milkers would get out, and we would then have an almighty scrum to catch it, put it back and get the right goat. Once they had finished their ration of feed they wouldn't allow us any more milk. Rosemarie was chief milker. It was a long time before I was anything like proficient at milking and I invariably ended up giving them twice the ration, and I still got only half the milk!

When we took the Billy Boys to the butcher we asked him to let us have the skins back as we intended to try our hand at curing them ourselves. The butchers were two brothers. A funny pair of old boys. They were very old-fashioned couple. Their buildings were very basic and would certainly not come up to modern hygiene standards. And contacting them was always difficult as they didn't even have a telephone. We were told we could contact them by phoning their neighbours two doors down, but we thought we'd be better off making our arrangements face to face.

When I opened up the sacks in which the skins were returned the first thing I saw was a pair of ears. I shut the sack up again quickly thinking the butcher had sent back the entire skins including the heads! It was an hour or so before I plucked up the courage to look again, and I was thankful to find the heads were not there. There was only part of the ear still attached to one of the skins.

The process of tanning involved stretching the skin, carefully removing any remaining particles of meat that might still be there, and then painting the skins with paraffin each day. At least, this was the easiest way for the amateur. There were more toxic chemicals for a more professional job. However, we found the meat had not been well butchered and there was an excessive amount of meat still attached to the skin, which made the job more difficult than it might otherwise have been. They were not good skins for our first attempt at tanning. In any case we didn't make a good job of it, and gave up. In retrospect what we should have used the skins for if we had been successful I don't know.

We learned a local health food shop was looking for a new supplier of goat's milk. When we approached them, they were delighted and said they couldn't get enough and they'd be able to sell all we could produce. We thought we'd hit the jackpot first time. This called for another goat!

And so we bought Brolly, a great hairy Toggenberg with a mottled light-brown coat and a rather domineering character. She used to tyrannise poor Sophie, Rosy and the Billy Boys, although she never got the upper hand over Lin, who was quite clearly 'senior goat'.

Brolly was quite a character. She used to go to bed on the rabbit hutch, happily chewing away at the felt roof. That is until the hutch fell apart under her weight, thankfully without George or Honey inside. One time when Rosemarie was taking Brolly to the billy goat, she was quite entranced by the Christmas lights as they drove through the local town. Rosemarie had a Citroën 2CV at the time, which, with the rear seats removed, made an excellent 'goatmobile'. It was especially useful as the goats could stand up in the car – in any of the other vehicles we used they had to spend the journey lying down. Brolly looked from side to side glancing at the colourful lights obviously quite enjoying herself.

The goats became quite used to their shelter in the paddock for when it rained. There was always some bitching, biffing and biting of bums when all they could do was stand in the shelter waiting for the rain to stop. On one occasion Brolly forced poor Sophie out of the shelter into the rain, and Sophie ended up catching a chill, for which we had to call out the vet. Not only was Brolly causing aggravation, but now she was costing us money as well.

Brolly was already in milk when we bought her, so we went back to the health food shop. Yes, they said, they'd have twenty pints a month. Twenty! That wasn't even a pint a day. What a let down! And what were we going to do with all that extra milk?

We decided breeding Angora goats for their fleeces was going to be the next up-and-coming business. But there was a slight problem there. We couldn't afford to buy a purebred Angora as the price was at a premium. A single goat could cost two or three thousand pounds. The alternative was to 'grade up'. If we were to cross a dairy goat with an Angora and put their offspring to an Angora, after five generations we would end up with a purebred. It would take several years, and we would need to have a female from each mating, but we decided to give it a go.

So when she next came into season I took Sophie to an Angora buck. Arranging a goat's love life was a new experience for me. I had to hold Sophie, on her lead, whilst the buck sniffed around her rear quarters and – er... – well, did what he was supposed to do.

The lady owner, Joan, who we knew only slightly, laughed:

'I don't know what my mother would say if she could see me doing this with a strange man!'

As it was, her mother couldn't see us. In fact, even if she had, I doubt she would have realised what was going on as she suffered from dementia. Joan, poor lady, worked nights as an auxiliary in an old peoples' home, and looked after her mother and the animals during the day. If she wasn't mucking out goats, pigs or cattle, she was mucking out her mother or the members of the home.

To add to the comedy, Angora goats are comparatively small animals and Sophie was quite tall anyway. So we had to find somewhere where the buck was at a higher level than she was.

After the event, we went inside to see to the paperwork and have a cup of tea, and then we went outside again to repeat the performance – just to be sure!

Five months later Sophie produced three fine kids, a male, who we named Gozo, and two females, Polo and Noddy. They had the finest fleeces I have ever seen on a first cross Angora – but then I do admit to being just a little biassed.

Despite her faults, Brolly clearly had a strong maternal instinct. When Sophie was raising her three kids, they would often go to sleep by the hedge, and Sophie would wander off with the others. When the babies woke up wanting a feed, they'd cry out for their mum. We would see both Sophie and 'Auntie' Brolly running across the paddock towards the kids, returning their calls, with their udders flopping from side to side as they ran, and Sophie's ears flapping up and down. It was quite a sight.

We sold Brolly soon after that as we had no need for all the milk. We had by then put up a 'Goats Milk For Sale' sign in the front garden. That and word of mouth attracted one or two private customers for the milk, and we also sold some to a local farm shop. But it didn't amount to many pints a month, and we were not going to get rich at twenty-five pence a pint!

Sophie never really settled down.

'She's driving me to distraction,' complained Rosemarie. 'She's noisy and neurotic, and a disruptive influence on the others. There's nothing we can do with her. We've tried everything. If she's out she wants to go in, and if she's in she bawls to go out. It's not fair when I'm working. She'll have to go.'

I knew she was right, particularly that it was not on for her to have to put up with Sophie's complaining when she was trying to sleep during the day. But I was fond of Sophie in a funny sort of way – she seemed to be a bit of a lost soul.

'We can't sell her,' I said hopefully, realising it would be unfair, both on Sophie and any new keeper, to have passed on the problem to another goat keeper.

'No,' Rosemarie replied. 'The hunt can have her.'

Not that we supported hunting, but the local hunt kennels did offer a valuable service to livestock farmers by putting down and carting away for free any sheep or goats.

Sadly, then, and very reluctantly, that was Sophie's fate. At least her kids were weaned by then, and they didn't even notice their mum had disappeared.

On the whole, goats are quite intelligent creatures. Gemma, I guess, was the exception that proves the rule. She was a black and white Anglo Nubian. She had very unusual and pretty markings, but always seemed to be sixpence short of a shilling.

She was last at almost everything. The other goats would be well into their feed before Gemma realised it was feeding time. Out in the paddock we would often see her gazing vacantly into space, apparently contemplating the mysteries of the universe, oblivious of the fact that the rest of the herd had by then made their way to the other end of the field. When she realised they'd gone, she would gallop down the field in her rather ungainly fashion to catch up with them, calling out, 'Wait for me, wait for me.'

Despite her apparent retardation, though, she did seem to know what was expected of her when we took her to the billy. In fact, she didn't want to come home!

When Gemma kidded, Rosemarie had gone off to work, leaving me to be midwife. It was about ten o'clock at night when she started. Like a nervous father-to-be I kept going outside to the stable to see if there were any signs of the impending birth and returning indoors when there was not.

When the first kid started to arrive, I helped her by pulling it off. I then had to ensure its nostrils were clear of mucus so it could breathe, and sprayed its navel with iodine. It was her first kidding and she seemed a little bemused by it all, not knowing quite what to do. I left her licking off her first born and went inside for a while and rang Rosemarie at the hospital to report on progress.

When I went out again, there were signs of a second arrival. I helped with that birth too, and I tried to make sure that both the kids knew where to look for their milk, and then left her to it.

I checked them all again before going off to bed and everything seemed to be fine. Imagine my surprise, though, when I checked her the following morning to find there were now three kids. There seemed nothing further for a seasoned goat midwife to do apart from spraying its navel, so I went off to work leaving a note for Rosemarie for when she got in half-an-hour later.

Somewhere along the line – 31st May 1988 to be precise – we bought Kiwi, who we had previously borrowed from Maureen to baby-sit Sophie. Although she was a very quiet and peaceful goat, she was not without a trick or two up her sleeve, and she was already about six years old when we bought her. Rosemarie took her to the same stud goat as Gemma and she produced twins within a couple of weeks of Gemma kidding.

We sold Gemma's three kids and one of Kiwi's, keeping the other one, who we named Daisy May. We were lucky that year in that we didn't even have to advertise the kids for sale. They just disappeared. Someone seemed to know someone who wanted a goat. It wasn't always like that, however, and we were always concerned they should go to good homes. Goats, perhaps more than any other domestic animals, often seem to be bought for the 'wrong' reasons, kept in poor conditions, and end up having a miserable existence. And we didn't want ours ending up that way.

Since we didn't need all Kiwi's milk – not that she gave a lot anyway – we let her and Daisy May graze together during the day so Daisy could suckle. But we kept them apart at night so we could take some milk from Kiwi in the morning. It saved us having to bottle feed Daisy, which made life in that respect a lot easier. Anything that could save us having to bottle feed was definitely a 'good thing' as far as we were concerned. Once she was weaned, we were able to let Daisy share the stable with her mum. They were inseparable. Even when she was fully grown we used to find the two of them curled up together when we came down in the mornings.

When she was about eighteen months old, we put Polo to an Angora buck. It was Rosemarie's turn this time, and it turned out to be a rather uneventful occasion. Polo produced two kids – a male and a female. We kept the female, naming her Sophie after her granny, and sold the male together with his mum. It was difficult to part with Polo, but we knew we would not be able to keep all our first, second and subsequent Angora crosses when our aim was to breed a pure Angora.

So now we had our second cross Angora. Sophie was a funny little thing, very full of the joys of life. She was surprisingly gentle, taking her bottle without giving us the bruises or cut fingers we usually received when bottle feeding. And, of course, she had the most superb fleece. She was very playful and would run up and down on top of our wood pile in the Tringle as sure-footed as if she belonged there. Polo had been something of a tomboy when she was a kid and it looked as though Sophie II was going to take after her mum in this respect. Since we had sold her dam, we had to bottle-feed her and – of course – give her extra care and attention.

Sadly, we never actually managed to get an angora fleece for Rosemarie to spin and knit up. Although after a few years it occurred to us to let the goats stay out in the field day and night during the summer, they had to come in at night during the winter. This meant the fleeces became matted with hay seeds and straw from their stable. So ended our dream of making our fortune with Angora goats.

On one occasion a farm lorry deposited part of its load of Brussels sprouts on the verge opposite Dorothy's petrol pump. Once we heard the news we lost no time in going up the road and filling as many sacks as we could with sprouts for the goats. And then we took Lin for a walk up the road to collect up those we had missed.

Another year our friend John let us have the remains of his sprout field. It was usually Rosemarie's job to take the van and fill it with the spent sprout plants. When she arrived home it was mayhem. On hearing the van's return Lin and the others jumped up at the stable door and started calling for their special treat.

And the year after that Clive offered us his failed field of cabbages.

Such treats were much appreciated by the goats, but their stable was not a pleasant place to be near for the rest of the evening!

Dear old Lin would frequently return from the field in the evening with a distended stomach, a mild form of bloat. It happened so often we referred to her as 'bloaty goat'. It was never sufficiently bad to warrant calling out the vet, but we used to have to administer a 'first aid' treatment in the form of a spoonful of cooking oil, which had the effect of lubricating the stomach and allowing the gases to escape.

The poor old dear also suffered from a form of rheumatism. She coped with it for several years, but we eventually sought veterinary help. The vet gave us little encouragement, just putting the condition down to her age, and sadly, after a further period we had to have her put down.

Luckily Rosy inherited Lin's calm and friendly temperament. She loved being the centre of attention and would always come over for a stroke when we went out to the field. On one occasion when we had a visitor, we were walking across the field together and Rosy came up behind him and sidled up to him. For a moment he looked rather put out until he looked down to see it was Rosy looking up at him with an expression as if to say, 'Hello, I'm Rosy. Do you want to give me a stroke?' Silly? Well, maybe it was daft to imagine the animals had 'human' tendencies. But then again, perhaps not.

She also had a rather jealous streak, though. Whenever we made a fuss of one of the others, she would come over and interpose herself between us and the current object of our affection. At times she could be particularly spiteful. If she thought one of the others was getting too much of our attention, she would bite the other's ear.

Rosy had one bonus for us. Well, it could be something of a mixed blessing. She was a maiden milker, which meant she gave some milk without having had a kid, and she first came into milk when she was about nine months old. She only gave a pint or so a day, but it had its uses.

One day we sold Noddy to a girl who had looked after goats at school, so we were one goat 'down'. That evening we took Rosy for boarding with a billy a few miles away, as we had never been able to catch her in season – we had missed her the previous year and didn't want to be caught out again. Another one gone. The following day the girl, apparently pleased with Noddy, decided she'd like company for her and so we sold her Gemma too. The remaining goats seemed to be rather alarmed to see their numbers dwindling so rapidly and looked apprehensive whenever we went near them.

About two weeks later Rosy still hadn't returned and Kiwi had come into season. So Rosemarie took her to the same stud. When she got there Rosemarie was told our normally calm and placid Rosy had jumped out of every pen she had been put in. She had finally ended up in one with a pony, where she had been left. We could hardly believe it. Rosy had never jumped anything at home.

On her arrival Kiwi seemed pleased to see Rosy and we imagined their conversation.

'So this is where you are. We wondered where you had got to. Are Noddy and Gemma here too?'

'No, I've looked in all the pens. I don't know where they can have gone. I hope mum's here to take me home.'

Kiwi stayed overnight and Rosy stayed a further night, too, and Rosemarie went to fetch them home together the following morning. Rosy was not her usual friendly self for several months after she came home. She refused to talk to us. Before she went away she would always answer us with a little bleat whenever we called her name, but she was having none of that now. And she didn't seem to want us to make a fuss of her.

We had put three goats – Rosy, Kiwi and Polo – in kid that year. At least, we thought we had. After all the expense of boarding her and feeding her up, Rosy failed to deliver the goods! She had been given the choice of three willing and able billies, and the stud owners had even resorted to giving her hormone injections to encourage her to come into season – with our agreement, of course. But it was all to no avail. Kiwi, too, failed us. And, as a half-Angora, Polo was not a milker anyway.

This meant we would have no milk for a whole year and we'd have the additional expense of feeding them for no output. Luckily Rosy came to our rescue, coming into milk again without having had a kid. She still produced only about a pint a day, but it was sufficient for most of our needs. It meant we would have none to sell, and there'd be no excess with which to make yogurt. And it was going to be an expensive way of getting our milk!

The following year was worse still. After the expense of trying to get Rosy in kid the previous year we decided not to try again. We had sold Kiwi and had no luck getting Daisy May in kid. Rosy, bless her, gave us about half a pint every three days.

As luck would have it, we spotted an advert for goats for sale in the local paper. An elderly lady who clearly loved her goats was having to sell up due to her failing health. Mrs Dunhill was only able to get about with the help of two walking sticks, and it was clear she had been unable to tend her animals herself for some while. It seemed her husband had eventually had enough of doing so. She had sold two of her four goats, one of which had recently kidded and one that was due to kid that day. She didn't want to sell her favourite, which was the mother of one of those she had sold and the grandmother of the other. But she wanted to let her go to a good home on loan.

Without realising it we obviously passed the test as Mrs Dunhill asked if we would take Kady on loan. It was a great honour as she clearly adored Kady. She asked if we thought she was beautiful to which we dutifully replied in the affirmative, but in truth I found her looks quite ordinary and Rosemarie thought her ugly! She was rather nondescript in appearance, of crossbred ancestry, and with a long-haired coat, white and brown in colour.

As Kady was 'senior goat' at Mrs Dunhill's we wondered whether she or Rosy would win the position at our place.

There was quite a bit of argy bargy when we got Kady home. In the end Rosy won. Kady seemed too laid-back to care. So long as she got her food she wasn't too bothered about herd politics.

Kady was already milking, which, after all, is what we wanted her for. She had been milking for a year already so the following year we put her in kid again.

But Kady was not at all keen on the process of giving birth to, nor of looking after, her babies. She didn't like them to suckle and barely took any notice of them. We had to make sure they got enough milk, especially as we wanted some of Kady's milk for ourselves. Eventually we thought it easier to rear them by bottle. Given our previous experiences of bottle feeding that was saying a lot! But that way we could be sure they were getting enough feed, and Kady was greatly pleased with the arrangement.

However, Kady was quite remarkable in one respect, which was that she continued in milk year after year without being put in kid. Anglo Nubian goats frequently manage to go for two years, but we had never heard of a goat of any breed that went on and on like Kady. Perhaps it was her dislike of kids. Every winter she would have a period of two or three weeks when she didn't want to eat much, whatever we might try to tempt her with. No doubt it was her body telling her to stop for a while. So we stopped milking her for that period – except to relieve the pressure on her udders – and she would soon return to her usual self.

Sadly, as well as inheriting Lin's calmness, poor old Rosy also acquired her arthritic condition. When she was still only six years old – younger than Kady – we had to have her put down, never understanding what the problem was. Although they had never got on, Kady seemed to miss Rosy. But only for a couple of days, after which she settled down quite happily to be a lone goat.

Rosy's failure to get in kid was a mystery to us, but it seems they can be prone to hormonal imbalances. One of Maureen's goats was a billy of unknown pedigree.

What she wanted to keep a billy for we couldn't imagine. No beating about the bush, billy goats stink. They 'spray' themselves – with what I'll leave to your imagination. Apparently it is supposed to make them attractive to the females. But to the human the result is quite offensive! Anyway, we were surprised when Maureen announced one day that her billy was giving milk! It seems that such a condition is not as uncommon as we at first thought. And, if I believed in coincidences, I might have found a little uncanny the request in the following month's Goat Society newsletter by a vet at an agricultural college asking members to provide details of any milking male goats for a thesis he was writing.

Early one afternoon, quite early on in our goat keeping career, Rosemarie asked quite unexpectedly, 'Do you want to go up to bed, or shall we go and see Maureen's new kids?'

Such was my fascination with baby goats that without hesitation I replied, 'Ooh, lets go to Maureen's!'

Oh, well. As they say, it takes all sorts. Perhaps it's not just goats that have trouble with their hormones from time to time.

4 Sheep

'Come on,' I called irritably. 'We've got all those woolly bastards to do before dinner. You said you were ready ten minutes ago.'

'I'm coming!' retorted Rosemarie. 'I had to get the syringes and vaccination ready. Why do we always fall out over the sheep?' she moaned, and then added, 'You're always in a hurry to get it over with.'

'We've only got eight sheep,' I said disparagingly, 'but you'd think it was a flock of a couple of hundred the time it takes us.'

'I've just got to get the marker,' announced Rosemarie, as she came out of the house and headed for the stables. I bit my lip. A minute later, 'Okay, I'm ready now.'

'Right, I've got the pen all ready. You stand there and I'll chase them all in,' I suggested.

'We'll never do it that way,' came her riposte.

'We'll never get it done at all if we don't get started,' I replied. 'Do you have a better suggestion?'

'No... But...'

'Well, no "buts". Let's try my way and if it doesn't work we'll try something else.' A few moments later, with all the sheep penned, 'There, that wasn't so bad was it?' I puffed.

'I suppose you think you're clever,' was all the response I got.

Our first sheep were four orphan lambs, two rams and two ewes, from the farm of a prominent local retired politician.

There are many terms used by farmers for lambs that have, for one reason or another, to be reared by hand, not all of them polite. Pet lambs, cade lambs, tame lambs or Rosemarie's term 'nibbies' are perhaps the more printable ones. Most farmers find them a lot of trouble and sell them off very cheaply.

Our two ram lambs were destined for the freezer, and the ewe lambs were to be the first of our breeding stock. We were very proud of our two girls, Emma, a Texel cross, and Mopsy, a Suffolk. As they were so young we had to feed the four lambs by bottle – 'tittie bottle' as it became known. They needed feeding four times a day for the first four months or so. And, for the first week, we had to get up in the middle of the night for a fifth feed. Did I say 'we'? Well, yes, I did do my share to begin with.

Hand rearing four hungry lambs was quite an undertaking. With just two bottles it was a bit like juggling. We would end up with two – or even three – little mouths desperately trying to get a suck from a single bottle as though their lives depended on it – which, of course, they did. They weren't to know they would get their fair share if only they were patient. Often if we looked away for a moment there would be a different nose at the teat-end of the bottle when we looked back. And they could be very rough, almost knocking the bottle out of our hands. It was even more of a hazard when they started cutting their teeth!

One day Em got the scours – that is, 'the runs'. We attempted to cure the problem ourselves with the help of a veterinary book, but to no avail. So Rosemarie took her baby to the vet. She was a very proud mum when everyone in the surgery waiting room admired Em. It must have made a difference from the usual cats and dogs. But it was something of an embarrassment when the vet examined her and said she didn't have anything wrong with her other than she had probably been eating too much!

That autumn we purchased three Icelandic ewes. Rosemarie wanted some coloured sheep for their wool, and Icelandic sheep appeared to be ideal for the smallholder, being about half the size of most commercial breeds and thus much easier to handle. In addition they come in a variety of colours – black, white and various shades of brown and grey.

As well as rearing our own meat and raising lambs for sale, we wanted the sheep for their wool. Rosemarie had been taking lessons in hand-spinning and had her own spinning wheel. She was all set to shear, spin, and knit the fleeces of any sheep that got in her way.

We bought two purebreds, Vashti and Helga, and a quarter-Shetland, named Dessie. Vashti was a lovely deep brown – or moorit, to use the correct term – and was two years old. She had a deformity in that her jaw was undershot, that is her lower jaw was shorter than her upper jaw, so we would never be able to keep any of her offspring for breeding. Helga, two shades of dark grey, was four, and Dessie, a black one, a year old. We had a hundred-and-fifty-mile journey to bring them home, but they seemed quite content in the back of the car, leaving the occasional pile of 'currants', and they soon settled in to their new environment when we got them home.

The Icelandics had come from a delightful, but slightly eccentric, lady of some breeding somewhere in deepest Wiltshire, the Hon. Mrs Ffollett. She had a flock of about seventy Icelandic sheep, each of whom she knew by name, and our three came complete with their pedigrees.

Although she appeared not to be particularly wealthy, it transpired she also owned a nearby racing stable. She sheared all the sheep herself by hand and had a room in her house full of fleeces all bagged up and labelled. She used to spin the fleeces and knit them up into jumpers, which her daughter sold in her Chelsea craft shop.

Rosemarie couldn't resist buying one or two fleeces – of colours she didn't already have, you understand. We spent a couple of hours looking around, and could have stayed talking with her for hours, but we had to get home with our ewes.

Our first attempts at catching the sheep must have looked hilarious to anyone who might have been watching. For us at the time it was exasperating. Our aim was to chase them from the paddock into the Tringle. It sounded easy, and it would have been a lot easier had the gate been in a corner rather than in the middle of one side of the field. We tried to herd them through the gate, Rosemarie taking one side and me the other. Several times we had all of them bar Dessie in the Tringle, but Dessie was just wilful and watched us from the far end of the paddock with her black gipsy eyes. After half an hour we gave up frustrated.

The following day my parents arrived for a visit, and so there were four of us jumping up and down and flapping our arms. Again we managed to catch all but Dessie. Eventually we decided that it was better than none.

It was some time afterwards – and after we had sold our prodigal sheep – we found the easiest way to catch them was with a bucket of food. It sounded almost too obvious, but it wasn't a method mentioned in any of our smallholding books.

Meanwhile I had become a dab hand with a shepherd's crook. On one occasion I nearly lost my prey, but a quick rugby tackle stopped the ewe getting away and I landed up on my back clutching my victim to my chest with its four feet waving in the air. It wasn't that we wanted to catch the sheep for the fun of it or for the good of our health, but rather that it was important to be able to catch them when needed as we had regularly to worm them, trim their feet, check them for maggots, vaccinate them, or for the annual shearing.

Our first year with the sheep we had five ewes but no ram. Our friends with the Angora goat buck happened also to have an Icelandic-cross ram, and so we took our 'girls' for a six-week holiday with Neil – the ram. We went to fetch them home a few days before Christmas, during the police anti-drink-drive campaign. The sheep were loaded into the back of the company car. I had a new car by then, an estate, chosen for the purpose.

We were stopped near home in a random check. I stopped the engine and wound down the window and a young WPC asked:

'Have you been drinking, sir?'

Before I could answer, a voice from the back said, 'Baaa.' It was our Em.

The WPC stepped back, visibly shocked.

'Oh... I, er... didn't realise. I'll... just check, er... your tax and tyres.'

The poor constable almost ran round the car, glanced at the tyres and tax disc, and wished us a safe journey. She didn't notice that Rosemarie, who had been turned round in her seat trying to stop the ewes coming forward in the car, was not wearing a seat belt. In fact I wondered if she even noticed whether I had a tax disc.

We thought of hiring a JCB and a skip, removing all the rubble where the mound was in the paddock, and restoring the spring. It would have made a lovely pond and would have saved us having to carry out buckets of water each day for the animals to drink. However, after our first mild and very wet winter, the paddock was very wet under foot and we found the mound to be a useful haven for the sheep to keep their feet dry. So, despite its untidy appearance, we decided to let it stay.

We had mixed fortunes at lambing time the following spring. Emma produced two babies at least ten days premature and we had not been expecting them so early. She lambed in the early hours on a cold and wet day, and by the time we had got up and discovered the lambs they were already dead.

We took the bodies away for later burial, but poor Em kept wandering back to the spot where she had lambed, crying pitifully. It was heart rending. In an attempt to pacify her and give her some lambs to raise, we bought two orphan lambs and tried to get her to accept them. We rubbed the backs of the dead lambs over the orphans to give them the smell of her own lambs. Some shepherds skin the dead lambs, putting the skins, like coats, over the orphans. But we didn't feel up to doing that. Another option is to use a 'fostering crate'. which is a contraption that allows the foster lambs to suckle, but restricts the ewe's movement so that she can't reject them. It doesn't always work even then, but we didn't have one anyway. As it was, we failed. Perhaps we just didn't try hard enough. Or maybe Em was too smart. Whatever it was Em rejected the lambs, and so we ended up having to bottle feeding them both!

Mopsy produced two lovely ewe lambs. She was having a difficult time with her birth and so Rosemarie called out the vet. We were always careful about calling for the vet. Not only was there the worry of the expense – farm visits didn't come cheap – but it was frustrating if there turned out to be nothing wrong, or something we could have sorted out ourselves. Or if there was nothing the vet could do either. In this case Rosemarie would not have been able to do anything herself. Me? Well I was at work anyway. It turned out Mopsy had ringwomb, which is when the cervix doesn't open properly. The vet was able to get the lambs off, and neither they or their mum seemed any the worse for their experience.

Helga and Dessie each produced only one lamb – Helga, a male and Dessie, a female. And Vashti produced twin ram lambs. She, too, lambed unexpectedly outside in the cold and wet, in the early hours of the morning. When we found them, both her lambs were alive but poorly. We took them and mum into a stable, and dried off the lambs with a hair drier. But sadly we were too late to save one of them.

After several months of indecision we had named all the lambs. Mopsy's were named Jean and Meryl, after two friends in Devon, Helga's boy was called Magnus and Dessie's girl, Eli. We always gave the Icelandic lambs Icelandic names, and even went to the trouble of getting a book about Iceland from the library in order to get sufficient names for them. Vashti's boy was the exception. Knowing we couldn't keep him because of Vashti's deformity, we simply named him Buster.

Sadly, Mopsy caught pneumonia that summer. We called out the vet, who told us it was impossible to tell what had caused it. He suggested it was probably brought on by the stress of the heat and change of pasture, but it was only a guess. Sheep seem to be so keen to keel over and die, anyway. We had recently moved them out from the paddock into the back field. But why sheep should become stressed by having lush new pasture was something of a mystery to us. That they might get bloat or the runs, yes. But, stress?

Anyway, the vet prescribed antibiotics – well, they always seem to prescribe antibiotics! At the time he told us nothing about the condition or her chances of recovery, and we didn't have the sense to ask. On further enquiry the senior partner told us Mopsy's chances of recovery were slim.

Although she fought hard – for a sheep, that is – it was clear that she wasn't going to recover. After about three or four days we had her put down. We assumed that as she had put so much into rearing her lambs, she had little energy left for herself. It was a difficult decision, and we were particularly sad to lose one of our first ewes.

Unlike the goats the sheep stayed outside all day every day, unless one was ill or when a ewe was lambing. The stables were not ideal for sheep used to the great outdoors all year round, as they were enclosed and had rather poor air circulation.

At lambing time the ewes stayed outside until they showed signs that they were due to lamb. That is, they had an enlarged udder and later started to look for somewhere away from the others to have their lambs in peace. At that stage they were easy to catch and didn't seem to mind very much being separated from the rest of the flock.

We would put the ewe into one of the stables and let her give birth inside. There would usually be one or two stables available for lambing. If not, we had to empty one hurriedly. We would either wait up until she lambed or get up at intervals during the night until she gave birth and then help out if needed. I say 'we' but in truth it was usually Rosemarie who got up in the middle of the night. The ewe and lambs remained inside for a couple of days before we let them out again with the rest of the flock.

When they were let out with the rest, all the other ewes would come over to see the new arrivals. Just like mothers in a maternity ward. Whoops, sorry! There goes another sexist remark!

The lambing season was always an exciting time. Despite having to get up at odd times of the night, all the worry and the deaths, it was exciting to be part of the process of new lives.

During lambing one year we were just getting into bed when we heard the distinctive call of Vashti. We ignored it for a while, thinking she was just calling to her lambs to hurry along. But when it continued, we realised all was not well and so we both got up, got dressed again, picked up the torch and went outside to investigate. We found her walking back and forth, looking for and calling to her lambs. Each time she returned to the place where, evidently, she had last seen them. We looked around for a while and couldn't find them for ages. Eventually we found them asleep, sheltering in a cranny, quite oblivious to the fretting of their mum.

Another time I got up to visit the bathroom at about two in the morning. It was a bright moonlit night, and I must have sensed rather than heard something out of the ordinary. I went downstairs and opened the back door to see Em's two lambs running, jumping and skipping up and down on top of the mound in the paddock having the time of their little lives. The rest of the sheep were looking on, apparently as bemused as I was.

The following year we bought an Icelandic ram from Mrs Ffollett. His name was Eddo. He was my fortieth birthday present to Rosemarie. Now there can't be many women who can say they had a ram for their fortieth birthday. But then, perhaps there aren't many women who would actually want a ram for a birthday present!

He was very quiet all the way home, standing in the back of the van and letting out just the occasional quiet, but deep, 'baaa'. He was a beautiful deep brown moorit, the same colouring as Vashti, and was very quiet and affectionate. At least he was for several years.

Eddo had a lovely pair of horns. They were a fine shape, and he looked quite handsome in them. They were also handy for when we wanted to hold him for worming, injections or feet clipping. Unfortunately, after a few years, we found one of the horns was growing ever closer to his eye and we would have to do something about it before it got too close. We had seen a couple of rams at market whose horns had actually been allowed to grow into their eyes. It was a ghastly sight, and I feel quite queasy just thinking about it now. At the time neither the farmer nor the auctioneer seemed to be bothered. Nowadays a farmer would be prosecuted for causing suffering, and the auctioneer would refuse to accept an animal for sale if it was obviously ill or injured.

We arranged to take Eddo to the vet to have part of his horns removed. We were told the process involved cutting off part of the horn using something resembling a piece of cheese wire. It didn't sound very pleasant.

While we were waiting we heard one of the vets say, with some trepidation, 'We've got a ram to do this afternoon.'

He needn't have worried. The dear old boy stood throughout the operation as good as gold. The vet even commented on how docile he was, and decreased the amount of anaesthetic he would need to use accordingly. Unfortunately the vet had great difficulty administering the local anaesthetic and had to make numerous attempts to stick the needle in Eddo's head around each horn. Poor old Eddo's head must have felt like a pincushion.

When we got him back into the van, he started to eat the carrots Rosemarie had bought for our supper, but after such an ordeal how could we deny him a little treat? Later that evening, presumably when the anaesthetic had worn off, we found him grinding his teeth in pain. He soon recovered, though, even if he looked a little strange with his cut off horns. They looked rather like a pair of sawn-off shotguns. We hoped it wouldn't cramp his style when tupping time came round that autumn.

Eddo could sometimes be quite a character. One year he only had three ewes. Poor chap, it was something of an insult for a ram of his calibre. After a week or so he seemed to be getting quite ratty with them when none of them had come into season. One feeding time Rosemarie hung their hay net on the fence as usual. Eddo stood in front of the hay looking very cross and, as though in punishment, would not let the ewes near the hay.

On another occasion, Rosemarie saw Eddo try to mate with the cow when she came into season, taking a running leap at her, but not surprisingly missing by miles. He looked a bit bemused, but, not to be defeated, tried again... and again. Rather puffed and obviously disappointed he eventually decided to give up, much to the relief of the cow.

There were times when Eddo seemed almost human. He used to look at us quizzically on occasions. One day he stood watching Rosemarie with his head to one side. Rosemarie wondered what was wrong. Eventually she realised she had gone out to feed them with her hair rollers in, and he was looking at her as if to say, 'What have you got in your hair?'

Eddo took quite a shine to Polo, one of our first-cross Angora goats. When we attempted to put the goats out into the paddock with the sheep during the mating season he would follow her around the field sniffing at her and licking his lips. It all looked very funny, but he was in deadly earnest. Not wanting any 'shoats', we thought it best to keep the sheep and goats separate during this period.

Later in the season when it was safe for Polo, we started to find Rosy making up to Eddo. She rubbed her face against his horns and took mouthfuls of fleece from his back, apparently eating it. He seemed to enjoy the attention to begin with, but when she kept on, day after day, he obviously became rather tired of it. It was very amusing at first, but it soon became an obsession with her. She wouldn't leave him alone. When we let the goats out into the field in the mornings, Rosy would look round for Eddo and head straight for him. Poor boy, he got no rest. Rosemarie suggested she had an imbalance of hormones. It might also have accounted for her failure to produce any kids.

Whether he got fed up having only a handful of ewes, rather than the fifty or so he would have had in a commercial flock, we weren't sure. Whatever the reason, Eddo took a fancy to chasing Rosemarie whenever she went to see to the sheep. Sometimes he would get close enough to give her a biff up the bum. Although, to my shame, I teased Rosemarie about it once or twice, it was certainly not a laughing matter. Sadly, unless it stopped, Eddo would have to go.

We had been intending to sell Magnus. But we wouldn't be able to use Eddo on his own offspring, and therefore we would need another ram. So we decided to keep Magnus for a season. Eddo and Magnus got on really well together. Some friends had lost one of their Icelandic rams who had been in a fight with another ram, and, as a result, had died of a brain haemorrhage. We were lucky that Eddo and Magnus seemed to get on so well, but it warned us to be careful. As it happened, we kept Magnus for three years before selling him to a friend.

We didn't want to be totally reliant on others for transporting our sheep and so when I heard of a cattle trailer for sale at a local farm I jumped at it. It seemed to be in reasonable order, and the farmer claimed he had been using it himself until quite recently. The floor was in need of some repair, but it would be suitable for the sheep for one season at least. A towing hitch on the car completed the job.

We hadn't appreciated the amount of official paperwork that keeping a few sheep would entail. First, there were the movement records. Every animal moved on or off the farm had to be recorded. The trading standards department of the county council provided us with a book with carbon copies so we could send them a copy of our stock movements once a year.

Then there was the sheep dipping. There was a statutory period each year during which all sheep in the country had to be dipped in an attempt to eradicate sheep scab. We had to notify trading standards when we were going to dip, and they might turn up to ensure it was done properly. Each sheep had to be dunked for a full minute, so it was not unusual to see the official with a stop watch. And, so we were told, it was not unknown for the official to insist on a sheep being done again because it had only be held under for fifty-nine seconds! Such are the rumours about officialdom.

There were plenty of reports in the farming press linking organo-phosphate (OP) sheep dips with various complaints, including respiratory problems, flu-like symptoms and depression. Despite these, few people seemed to take the possible threat seriously and as a result the toxic solution would often get everywhere. Many farmers did not adequately protect themselves and would get drenched. And some farmers even threw in their sheepdog for good measure. It seemed like Pretty Dangerous Stuff to us.

We found a local farmer who had the equipment for dipping and was prepared to take in all comers for seventy pence a sheep. We arrived to find a vast assortment of sheep breeds. We'd never known there were so many flocks in the vicinity. At home we had loaded the trailer with our flock with comparative ease.

Then came the part I was dreading. Reversing the car and trailer. I could never get the trailer to go where I wanted it. I had got the hang of turning the steering wheel in the opposite direction when reversing with a trailer, but then straightening it up again proved more tricky. It took several attempts going backwards and forwards to get it near enough to unload the sheep.

We thought the men were rather rough in handling our sheep. Em's ears, normally quite perky, were droopy for several days afterwards. Rosemarie interpreted the 'ear language' and informed me Em was saying, 'How could you put me through that ordeal?'

Of all the days we didn't want it to rain, this was one of them. The poor old sheep would be soaked through with the dip and we wanted some dry weather to enable them to dry out. But it was not to be. We'd had the driest summer that most of us could remember and were suffering from drought, but it rained without stop all that day and most of the next. Our main concern was that they would catch pneumonia. Thankfully, though, our worries were unfounded. They all dried out and seemed to suffer no long-term ill effects.

Our second year of sheep dipping was another experience. We were without a car with a towbar then, and had to ask a favour of our farmer friend Jack. A friendly and helpful character, Jack was happy to do many things for the price of a couple of pints. He was around forty and at the time a bachelor. A jolly chap, he always seemed to find something to laugh about whatever the situation, and was invariably accompanied by his beloved Jack Russell bitch, Suzie.

We drove up to the farm where the dipping was being done to be greeted by a sight that belonged more to a bygone era than to the late twentieth century. Coming down the road towards us were three very large Suffolk sheep – a ram and two elderly ewes – pursued by two harassed women.

'Aye, that's a pair of big 'uns,' laughed Jack's mate.

'Them ewes is pretty large too,' jested Jack, and we all roared with laughter. For once Rosemarie was outnumbered, and the sexist joke went unchallenged.

We waited patiently while the ladies got their sheep through the farm gate. It transpired the sheep had escaped once and their owners had had to run up the road after them to fetch them back, hence the harassed look.

As we waited for our turn at the dip, we watched the others being dipped and chatted to one or two of the owners. As the big 'mama' Suffolk stood there recovering from her ordeal, dripping wet and trying to catch her breath, the ram saw his chance, jumped on her back and had his wicked way with her. The poor ewe looked as if that had been the last straw! No doubt, Jack would have a few tales to tell down the pub that night.

We weren't sorry when the law was changed so that annual sheep dipping was no longer compulsory. It was a lot of bother for small flock keepers like us, and had done very little in meeting its aim of eradicating sheep scab. And what those chemicals did to the meat and the environment is anybody's guess.

It is often said that sheep have but one aim in life and that is to die! It's true they certainly don't seem to have much will to live. They become stressed very easily, as we had learned with Mopsy, and are prone, like most animals, to a number of diseases. But when a sheep becomes ill it seems to have very little will to recover.

It was a dilemma for us whether or not to vaccinate the sheep against several diseases such as tetanus, braxy, blackleg and pulpy kidney. Although we made no pretence of being organic, our aim was to farm with as few artificial chemicals as possible. All our animal welfare books recommended preventative vaccinations, but given they were written by traditional vets perhaps that was not too surprising. Given we lost sheep that had been vaccinated, as well as some that had not, we were by no means convinced of the benefits.

Another affliction of sheep is maggots, or fly-strike. During the summer months sheep can be prone to these pernicious creatures. Flies lay their eggs in a mucky or wet part of the sheep's wool and when the eggs become larvae they start to burrow beneath the skin. They cause a lot of discomfort and will kill a sheep if not caught early enough.

Once again we could use chemical preventative measures, or treat the problem if and when it occurred. Given that we – or rather the sheep – usually succumbed to maggots at least once a year, prevention seemed the most judicious option. Even then we were sometimes caught out and had to cut away part of the fleece around the affected area, remove the maggots, and treat the area with disinfectant.

I used to tease Rosemarie that she was probably the biggest menace to the sheep. She worried about them a lot. It was a trick she had learned from her mother, always imagining the worst would happen. Somehow it was no great surprise when her fears were actually realised.

One of her concerns was that a sheep would get onto its back and would be unable to get back onto its feet. As a result it would almost certainly suffocate. This almost happened more than once with our Em. It would have to be her, with her large rump. On one occasion it was just a few months before she was due to lamb. Luckily Rosemarie found her in time and turned her up the right way. Had she not been around, Em would surely have died. But we were still concerned in case she should abort her unborn lambs. At least that fear was unfounded.

Another year, we were alerted to something by Eddo calling. He was in the paddock with Magnus, and Em and the rest of the girls were in the back field. Eddo had obviously noticed Em's predicament through the hedge and started calling for us to help. Rosemarie went out to investigate what Eddo wanted and eventually found Big Em upside down. Again she was in time to avoid a fatality.

Sheep

My birthday present from Rosemarie one year was a Gotland ewe lamb. We had become interested in the Gotland breed after reading about their fine fleeces in a farming magazine. They were slightly smaller than Icelandics and thus of even less interest to the commercial breeder.

We located a breeder, Mr and Mrs Harding, only a dozen miles away. They had a flock of almost two hundred sheep of a variety of unusual, if not rare, breeds, including Soay, Herdwick, North Ronaldsay, Badger-Faced Welsh Mountain, and several we had never even heard of. With all these different breeds, Rosemarie just had to have a couple of fleeces. As I waited patiently, I would be summonsed out of my daydreams with, 'Oh, Graham, just look at this one.' And, 'I've never seen one like this before!' Or, 'Isn't this an unusual colour?'

As well as the sheep, they had a few cattle, some ponies and a couple of hinnies.

'What are hinnies?' we chorused. We didn't like to admit we originally thought they were donkeys. I've always had a soft spot for donkeys but Rosemarie had no time for them at all, considering them to be useless creatures.

'They're a cross between a donkey and a pony,' Mr Harding explained, no doubt used to the question. And before we could say we thought that resulted in mules, he continued. 'A mule is the result of mating a female horse and a jack – that's a male – donkey, and it has the looks of a pony. A hinny is the result of a female donkey and a male horse or pony and looks more like a donkey. This pairing often doesn't take and as a result, hinnies are quite rare.'

The Hardings had a matching pair, which made them even rarer. They used them for driving, but, with all the work they had on the farm, their full time jobs, and showing their animals, we wondered how they ever found time for hinny driving.

Anyway, my little Gotland lamb was called Avril, although we always called her Gottie. She was a pretty, grey-fleeced sheep. She needed a little extra feeding up when we got her home due to a shortage of grass at the Hardings'. Gottie was rather timid to begin with, but she soon got used to coming for the bucket for her 'extras'. Before long she enjoyed being handled and once she got to know us would even come up to us and ask for a tickle on the chest. The brazen hussy!

As she got older, Gottie grew white round her eyes and mouth which gave the impression of her having been caught in the frost.

Shearing was another highlight of the year. In the first year we took our sheep to a local farm where there was a team of shearers who worked like a production line. They took about a minute and a half for each sheep, but were none too careful and one or two of our sheep came back rather badly cut.

In subsequent years, true to our hopes to be as self-sufficient as we could be, we decided to shear our own sheep. Rosemarie had some experience at the task and so she wielded the hand clippers whilst I held the victim still. Rosemarie attempted to shear them one year with electric shears, but to do this the sheep needed to be brought in from the field to the yard, where we had electricity. It seemed easier, after all, to use the hand shears and do the job in the field.

Sometimes after the ewes had been shorn, the lambs were unable to recognise their mums. They would go round bleating at each ewe in turn. Their mother, presumably glad for the respite in having her udders bumped, bruised and bitten, frequently didn't respond. As a result the lambs ended up weaning themselves a few months early.

5 Poultry

I had never thought of birds and poultry as being particularly interesting creatures. And our first acquisition, six point-of-lay hybrid pullets, did nothing to alter my view. We wanted to have our own eggs, and so we visited a local farm centre which had no end of different breeds of poultry. There was such a choice our heads were spinning. After much um-ing and ah-ing, we chose a common Rhode Island Red/Light Sussex cross, good reliable little layers. We bought half a dozen. They seemed particularly stupid birds, and would take fright at the slightest noise or movement. And they all looked much the same. In order to tell them apart we gave each one a leg ring of a different colour, and referred to them by the colour of their ring.

Ah, but it was exciting when we found their first egg. Every day when we went out to feed them we would check to see if there were any eggs. And when we found the first one we fought over who should cook and eat it. In the end, I seem to recall, we had half each! Those first six hens did us proud. Apart from a period during the first summer when they stopped laying for a few weeks, we had a constant supply of eggs for almost two years.

They lived in a mobile arc and run in the orchard, which we moved alternate days. It took several months to do a complete circuit of the orchard, so by the time we got back to where we started we reckoned the ground ought to have been clean and parasite-free again.

I have already said I thought the hens rather stupid creatures. The idea is to give them a nesting box in which to lay, and to put a china egg in the nest box to remind them where to lay their eggs. But we used to find eggs dropped anywhere – in their sleeping area, in the run itself, and occasionally even in the nest box.

Added to that was the fact that one or two of them started to eat their own eggs. Not only did this deprive us of the eggs that had cost us so much to produce, but it seemed to me a particularly sick form of cannibalism!

I came home from work one night to find a very excited Rosemarie. She had been to a local market and returned with a dozen Maran chicks, a broody coop, and what she thought was a Bantam hen and her eight chicks. We had been very keen to get Marans for their lovely dark brown eggs.

One friend later told us the Bantams were Jungle Fowl. Someone else told us they were Belgian d'Ucles, so what they really were we never did find out. However, whatever they were, Mum and babies were ensconced in the broody coop in the orchard.

We were stunned and upset the following morning, though, to find one of the JF chicks dead with puncture marks around its neck. Over the next few weeks we found several more of the chicks either dead or missing. It was very distressing, but we couldn't imagine what was killing or taking them. And we couldn't figure out how to stop it. There was no sign of a fox and we knew it wasn't our cats or we should have found some of the remains outside the back door! In any case neither a fox nor the cats could have got into the broody coop without burrowing into it – and I think we might have noticed that!

Meanwhile, the Marans were allowed to free range. It was not a great success, as they found their way into the vegetable plot and started to dig up any plant that was just becoming established. We had enough to contend with, what with the dry weather, moles and rabbits without our own hens as well. And when they started to lay we were never sure where to find the eggs! We discovered there were three hens and the rest were cockerels, and decided to keep the hens and one of the cocks, putting them into the arc and run vacated by the hybrid hens, and we would have the rest of the cockerels for the pot.

We bought a small incubator and hatched one batch of Maran eggs. We set fourteen eggs. They had to be turned twice a day and splashed with water. And we had to ensure that the temperature remained constant throughout the twenty-one days. Towards the end of the incubation period we became quite excited, and as we turned each egg we looked and listened for signs of them hatching. Once the first egg started hatching most of the rest followed pretty quickly. As each egg hatched, we put the chick under an infrared lamp for several days. It was difficult to judge the right temperature of the lamp, and we had to adjust the height of the lamp several times so it was warm enough but not too hot. Sadly, though, two of the chicks died. And some of the eggs didn't hatch at all.

We ended up with eight chicks, which we considered a very reasonable hatching rate, especially for our first attempt. Once they were a few days old, we put them outside in the broody coop. As the chicks grew, we let them out during the day to roam round the orchard. However, just like the adult birds they were very scatty and took fright at the slightest sound. As a result we christened them the morons.

My first attempt at killing a chicken for the pot is something I care not to remember, let alone write about. Suffice it to say it was not a great success for either party concerned. I didn't succeed on my first try, and I felt decidedly nauseous as I watched the chicken wander off looking a little bemused. It was a long while before I decided to have another go, and then only after I had acquired a suitable implement for the job.

One night, Rosemarie went out to put the Jungle Fowl, or whatever they were, to bed and returned dismayed.

'I can't find them, Graham.'

'Can't find who? What?' I replied, puzzled.

'The Jungle Fowl. I've looked everywhere. Come and help me look.'

'They've got to be somewhere,' I muttered, getting slowly out of my comfortable armchair.

I grabbed a torch, and together we looked all round the orchard. At the base of each apple tree, all round the chicken's arc and run, everywhere we could think of. Sure enough, there they were, gone. We began to think the fox had got them, but there were no telltale signs, and it seemed unlikely he'd have got them all in one go.

Having exhausted the possible options, we began to consider the impossible. I stood still for a while listening, and eventually I heard a faint 'cheep, cheep, cheep,' or two. I shone the torch in the direction of the sounds – into a nearby apple tree. There, to our surprise, were all the JF perched on the tree's branches. With great difficulty we managed to catch them all, lifting them one by one out of the tree and putting them back into their coop.

Thereafter the chicks put themselves to bed each night in the branches of the apple trees, and we would go out, collect them all up, and put them, squawking, back into their home for the night.

After a few weeks of this we began to think it would be safe to let them sleep the night in the tree. It was a sad mistake. One morning we came down to find a number of feathers, and Mum and all but one of the chicks gone. It was heartbreaking. It was also pretty foolish. Why had we assumed it would be safe? Too late, we realised it was probably rats that had been knocking off our JF.

We felt some sort of obligation to name the remaining chick and take extra care of her. She was duly named Speckledy – no prizes for guessing her colouring. I knocked together a small nesting box for her, which I mounted on the side of one of the remaining Poplar trees. She didn't seem to take to it and so I had to put her into it each night and put a door on so she couldn't get out. In the mornings we would open the door to let her out. Although we didn't like to cage her, we didn't want to lose her to the rats.

Unlike the rest of the chickens Speckledy did have character. We trained her to fly up onto the fence and eat out of our hands, and later she learned to perch on

Rosemarie's shoulder at feeding time. Sometimes she would let us stroke her, but if she thought we were getting too familiar she would let out a 'squawk' and give us a little peck.

After a few months we started finding eggs in her nest. They were small bluish ones. It was very exciting when we found the first clutch. We took them away, leaving just one to encourage her to continue to lay in the same place. After a further week or so she became broody and started to sit on her nest for most of the day. She would leave it only briefly each day to eat and drink. So we substituted a couple of Maran eggs for her infertile eggs in the hope she might hatch them. In retrospect it was probably not a very clever idea as the Maran eggs were so much bigger than Speckledy's own and she would have had great difficulty in turning them.

To our disappointment Speckledy was frightened off her nest by a magpie. It then promptly stole her eggs, and Speckledy never returned to her nest box after that. After her experience with the magpie, Speckledy used to sit on top of the Marans' run, eyeing up the cockerel. So after a while we thought it was time to find her a husband.

A friend of a friend wanted to get rid of a Jungle Fowl cock, but we could only have him if we took his mum as well. So we had them both. Mum was called Buttercup. Her son had no name and so we called him simply Son. Mum was a pretty dark golden colour; Son looked like the cockerel on the front of the cornflake packet.

Sometimes the cockerels seemed to have a competition. The Maran cock would crow, and Son would answer back. 'Cocky' would reply and they would go on like this until Rosemarie, fed up with the proceedings, chased them off threatening to cook the winner for Sunday lunch.

One morning Speckledy didn't come for her breakfast with Buttercup and Son. Always fearful of the fox, we assumed the worst had befallen her. But later in the day we heard her familiar, shrill 'squawk'. She had come for some food and didn't want to be kept waiting!

'Hey, Graham, Speckledy's here,' called Rosemarie in surprise. And then with relief, 'The fox hasn't had her.'

'What's she making all that noise for?'

'She wants her breakfast.'

'Cheeky little sod. Why doesn't she come when we're feeding the others?'

'I expect she's started nesting again.'

'Well I suppose we'd better find out where her nest is then.'

Next day the same thing happened. So when she had eaten, Rosemarie followed her surreptitiously into the orchard to try to see where her nest was. She returned after three-quarters of an hour.

'Where have you been?' I asked.

'Trying to see where Speckledy's got her nest,' she replied, sounding not just a little annoyed.

'What, all this time?'

'Yes! And don't ask me where it is 'cos I don't know!' Pregnant pause... 'I followed her into the orchard and made out I was busy. But she knew I was watching. She wasn't going to let me see where her nest was. She had three dust baths just to pass the time and led me a merry dance. Eventually, I went to fetch a bucket of water for the geese. When I came back Speckledy had vanished. Ooh, I'm that vexed!'

I roared with laughter.

'Oh I knew you'd find it funny!'

'You have to admit she got one over on you. And I just love it when you get "vexed" as you put it!'

In time we did find out where she was nesting. A couple of days later one of the cats inadvertently found and frightened her – and got an earful for his trouble!

The fox got Buttercup one night. All we found the following morning were a few feathers, but there was sufficient of a trail to see where he had got into the orchard. She and Son used to sleep at night perched on top of the Maran's run. We were none too happy with this arrangement, but try as we might, we could never catch Son to put them both somewhere safer. Even after dark, when it was quite easy to catch all the other chickens, we could never catch Son. Sad though it was to lose her, we didn't miss Buttercup much. We never got any eggs from her and she did nothing to earn her keep.

Several days before the fox came, Speckledy had gone missing again and we assumed she had nested yet again. But when we saw what had become of Buttercup, we assumed the worst for Speckledy. To our surprise and relief she appeared briefly that afternoon. And as luck would have it – or was it deliberate on her part? – I saw the direction in which she went, and it wasn't long before we discovered her nest behind the duck's house. That evening, expecting the fox to return, I filled in the gaps in the fence where 'Reynard' had got in the previous night, and put up a barricade around Speckledy's nest. Whether or not it would have stopped a determined fox is a moot point, but we didn't want to move her off her nest as she would stop brooding.

A few nights later, the fox must have returned because, although we found no signs of him, Son had gone missing. We hoped before he went he had mated with Speckledy, and the eggs she was sitting on were fertile. It seemed unlikely as we'd never seen them going out together. We had seen him playing mothers and fathers with Buttercup! But not with Speckledy. As time went by, it became apparent Speckledy's eggs were not going to hatch. The poor little thing refused to give up and she sat for at least two weeks beyond what would have been their incubation period. Son had obviously been too fond of his mum.

After that, Speckledy took to roosting in the apple trees again at night. We had almost forgotten about the fox and allowed Speckledy to put herself to bed each evening before dusk. Several months later, though, the fox must have returned for her. There were no signs of her, but we presumed she had got out of her tree too early in the morning. Poor little Speckledy, she wouldn't have made much of a meal. We missed her bright chatter and cheerful character about the place. Especially as Rosemarie reckoned she was teaching Speckledy to talk.

...Ducks are comical things –
As comical as you.
Quack!
They waddle round, they do
They eat all sorts of things,
And then they quack.

F W HARVEY

And eat all sorts of things, they do. But for the squeamish it's probably best if I don't mention that!

We obtained – from the proverbial friend of a friend – three ducks of different breeds. There were two females, a white one whom we named Dilys, and a brown, who was given the unfortunate name of Rubber, and the drake, which Rosemarie named Bumbly.

Sadly, we had no pond for the ducks and they had to make do with an old water trough in the orchard. When it rained they got particularly excited, congregating round the nearest puddle, ducking their heads and quacking as if conducting some ancient pagan ritual.

They were prolific egg layers, and what with our hens eggs as well we had more than we could eat ourselves or sell. So we decided to hatch one batch of duck eggs. We set about fourteen eggs, of which eight hatched. Much to our surprise, we found they were all females. Twelve eggs hatched, but we had three cot deaths and a fourth one died when it was quite grown for no apparent reason. Rosemarie found the duckling as though in mid waddle, with its eyes open, but quite dead. We had one of them for the pot, but there was not much meat on it, and so the others were reprieved – at least for a while.

We sold two for pets and kept the rest to raise eggs, though why we should have wanted more eggs when we couldn't sell them all, I can't imagine. Looking back I must sometimes question our sanity.

Their egg-laying habits were quite unusual to say the least. And very frustrating at times. In the mornings we would often find two or three in a nest in their hut, which was fine. But in the evenings when we went out to feed them, we would frequently find one or two just lying on the ground in the orchard. Sometimes one would be warm, as though it had been dropped the middle of whatever the duck was doing at the time. We found them in the strangest of places – beside their water bucket, in the orchard and even on the drive.

One of the ducklings became broody and made a nest for herself in their house. She had chosen the place where Rubber and a couple of the others had been laying their eggs. It seemed that no one had told her the facts of life, that if she wanted her eggs to hatch she would need a drake – rather surprisingly perhaps we had not seen Bumbly with any of the ducklings. She used to leave her nest a couple of times a day to eat, drink and stretch her legs, and would panic if we were not there to feed her.

One morning she left her nest when we let all the ducks out and she had her breakfast with the others. Rubber started to waddle back to the nest to lay her egg for the day. But the other duck – we had no name or other identification for any of the ducklings – didn't want anyone else laying in her nest and gave Rubber a race back to the house. She won and poor old Rubber had to find somewhere else to lay her egg.

If ours was anything to go by, drakes seem to be sex mad. When he was old enough, Bumbly started chasing the females to have his wicked way with them. Unfortunately for him, but much to our amusement, to begin with he couldn't quite get the hang of it. Following a bit of 'foreplay' he would climb onto the female and then promptly fall off onto his back with his wedding tackle waving, obscenely, in the air. Undaunted he'd then try again.

His sexual appetite seemed boundless, but it was eventually his downfall. On one occasion the ducks got into the front garden and wandered into the road, with the result that Dilys was hit by a car and was badly injured. We kept her apart from the other two and nursed her for a day or two, but she was unhappy being kept on her own and so we decided to put her back with the others. Despite her injuries, though, Bumbly insisted on his conjugal rights with Dilys – several times a day! When we found her dead the next day, we decided that Bumbly had had his chips – or to be more exact, we would have chips with Bumbly. We were not having sexual harassment on our farm!

Not long after we got the ducks, we were also given two geese – a gander, Hissing Sid, and his wife, who had no name but we decided to call Polly. Although he made a lot of noise – hence his name – Sid was quite a softy and I became very fond of him.

To begin with we had no house for them, and so they spent the night in one of the spare stables. It defies belief when I think of it now, but until we learned how easy it was to drive the geese, we used to pick them up and carry them into their stable! I carried Sid and Rosemarie carried Polly. We had a loan horse in the next stable at the time. One morning as I was carrying Sid out into the orchard, the horse was looking out at the goings-on. As we passed her stable Sid lunged out and, for no apparent reason, bit poor Neddy on the nose. Neddy was rather surprised but not hurt.

At feeding time we would call them, 'Sid and Polly, Sid and Polly,' and they'd come running, usually from the other side of the orchard, chattering excitedly. Sometimes, if they were in a hurry or overexcited, they'd flap their wings to propel themselves a little faster. On one occasion when they did this, Sid unintentionally took off and found himself flying in a rather ungainly fashion a few feet above the ground.

'Come and see this, Rose,' I called.

'Oh God. What does he look like?' she laughed. And then with concern, 'He's not going to be able to stop in time.'

Unfortunately Rosemarie's prediction was right. Sid had misjudged his stopping distance and flew just over the fence, ending up the other side in the paddock. He looked around him as if it was what he had intended all along, but it was clear he didn't seem to know how to get back. And he was missing out on his dinner. It obviously didn't occur to him to fly back, and so I had to walk round, pick him up and carry him back again. He seemed to know we were laughing at him. Was it just my imagination or did he look just a little embarrassed?

The first year, Polly hatched five goslings. It was something of a surprise when we – or rather Rosemarie – found the eggs. We had been expecting her to have been laying for a few weeks, and checked inside their house each day. But we had found nothing. One day Rosemarie was cleaning out their hut and to her surprise found a nest of about ten eggs. The first I knew about it was when I came home from work that evening to find a 'Goose Eggs For Sale' sign on the front lawn beside the drive.

Rosemarie took away all the eggs to encourage Polly to lay some more. She used to lay about one egg every other day. Each time she laid one we took it away until about the middle of March, when we started to leave them for her to hatch. Once she had enough, Polly started to sit.

We managed to sell most of the goose eggs that year – those we didn't eat ourselves. It seemed a lot of people were very keen on goose eggs and, at fifty pence each, they seemed to be prepared to pay a good price for them. Rosemarie used them herself in cakes, omelettes and for scrambled eggs. Some people who bought them apparently just wanted them to decorate.

We were pleased with Polly's hatching rate. She had been sitting on ten eggs and, as I've said, hatched five. According to one of our books, geese normally hatch only about a third of their eggs.

During incubation she hardly came off her nest, and she ate and drank very little. We were rather concerned that she was beginning to look a little scrawny, even though we understood this was perfectly natural. She turned her eggs religiously twice a day, and occasionally came off her nest to splash her underside with water so she would be able to keep the eggs moist.

It was exciting when they hatched. We heard a cheeping sound from inside the hut, but they stayed inside for several days. Whenever we tried to get a look at them, we were faced with a proud, hissing, mum and dad.

We kept one of the females, who we named Georgina after Rosemarie's boss at work, although we used to call her – the goose, that is, not Rosemarie's boss – Georgie for short.

We had intended to swap Georgie for an unrelated female so Sid would have a second wife. But somehow or another we never got round to swapping her, and we ended up the next year with Sid mating both Polly and his daughter. Sid obviously wasn't fussed.

Georgie layed her first egg on the dung heap. But for fear of the fox we took the egg away and tried to encourage her to lay inside the house. That way we would be able to shut them all up at night. However, we ran into trouble when the two females got their nests confused. They both started laying inside the house, and as a result we ended up with them hatching only three goslings.

On one occasion, after working one of her night shifts, Rosemarie got up mid afternoon and let Kyrie, her beloved Great Dane, out into the yard, whilst she brewed an extra strong mug of coffee. She had apparently forgotten the geese were also in the yard, but was soon reminded by the honking of the adult geese, and was horrified to see Kyrie attacking one of their number. Rosemarie dashed out into the yard, still wearing her bedtime apparel – just a tee shirt, which didn't even cover the bare essentials – and her slippers. In her haste to save the geese she had forgotten she was in full view of the road! Sadly, though, she was too late to save one of the geese.

To teach her a lesson, Kyrie was held still for Sid to reprimand her, which he did by biting her on the bum.

It might sound a bit cruel, but she had to learn. And it seemed to do the trick, as she took no notice of the ducks, geese and chicken after that. The goose wasn't wasted either, as we had it for dinner that weekend.

The geese used to play together as a family. Except for Brown Goose, that is. We were given Brown Goose by some friends, Warren and Jackie, who had decided to give up geese. They'd had three geese, all with highly original names – a gander, called Gander, and two wives, Brown Goose and Grey Goose. Their geese were attacked, and Grey Goose killed, by their dog. The experience had unhinged Gander who had attacked Warren, injuring him in the private parts. Warren had even had to go into hospital for a repair job after the attack. Gander got his comeuppance when the fox got him, before Warren got to him. That left Brown Goose all sad and alone, and so we said we'd have her. Sadly though, she wasn't readily accepted by our three. The females didn't want her and Sid paid her little attention. He didn't even want her for his conjugals. But she had company, and that, we felt, was better than being alone. In retrospect, though, perhaps it wasn't. She was even harassed by the sex-mad drake Bumbly.

The third year, we attempted to incubate some goose eggs. But we weren't very successful. Of the twenty eggs set, only one hatched. Most of the eggs oozed a sticky, smelly substance, and had to be disposed of carefully, deep at the bottom of the dung heap. We guessed they had probably not been fresh enough when we set them. We hatched them – or rather him – in the dining room, and, as we had done with the chicken, we put him under the infrared lamp. Every so often would go in and call to him.

'Gozzy, Gozzy.' To which we would usually get a reply, 'Wee, wee, wee, wee.'

We felt rather sorry for him all alone and so when he was a few days old we thought we'd see if the 'grownups' would accept him. Rosemarie took Gozzy out to the adult geese, and the result was most touching.

Sid and Brown Goose came over, honking excitedly. They made a great fuss of him, and then Sid showed Gozzy up onto the top of the dung heap, where Polly was sitting on her eggs, nudging him up with his head and beak, and encouraging him every step of the way. Polly lifted up her wing, and Gozzy went and nestled under it. It was an amazing and touching experience to watch.

For months afterwards we still used to call to Gozzy when he was in the orchard, 'Gozzy, Gozzy.'

'Wee, wee, wee, wee.'

Gozzy even brought out a new woman in Brown Goose. She was just as protective as Polly, lowering her head and hissing at us if we went too close to Gozzy. But it didn't last for long. Sadly, after Georgie hatched her three, Brown Goose became a gooseberry again.

One morning we came down to find a fox had tunnelled its way into the duck house, which at the time was home to the geese. We were gobsmacked. I hardly dared open the house. When I did, it was a horrific sight that faced us. Sid was dead, but the fox had been unable to drag his carcase through the hole it had made. Polly was in hysterics. A bag of nerves, she was wandering back and forth chattering to herself, splattered in blood and with a chunk taken out of her poor beak. Georgie was unharmed physically but rather distraught. It was clear that poor Sid had died trying to protect his female folk.

Not only were we sickened and upset at the sight, but we were also very angry with the fox. We wanted to get even.

We hatched our dastardly plan.

Knowing the fox would be back the following night, we decided that poor Sid should not die in vain. Using his carcase as bait we tied him to an intricate length of string which ran from the yard up through the bathroom window, and was attached to a bell just outside our bedroom.

Sure enough, we were woken in the small hours by a ting-ting-ting on the bell. We leaped out of bed and I grabbed my shotgun, which was already loaded and to hand, and ran downstairs.

The fox had gone.

The scenario was repeated several times that night. We wandered around half-clothed to see if the fox had hidden nearby in the orchard or the paddock, but every time there was no sight of it. It was probably lying low somewhere very close, watching. And no doubt laughing at us.

A similar exercise went on the following night before we eventually concluded the fox was too wily for us and gave up, burying Sid's carcase unceremoniously in the muck heap.

Poor old Polly and Georgie never recovered from their ordeal. There didn't seem anything we could do for them. We got no more eggs from either of them, and Polly seemed particularly distressed at having lost her mate. Given that geese usually keep the same mate for life she must have been especially upset. We eventually sold the pair to a family who intended to get a gander as well. We saw them from time to time when we passed their new home and they seemed very happy in their new life.

The geese we had hatched were intended for the pot. But they're not easy to pluck, are geese. The outer feathers are very tough – making ideal quill pens – and then there is another layer of under feathers (the down) and then the stubble. We often used to end up removing the final bits of stubble using a blow torch!

Rosemarie and I sat outside in the yard plucking the geese together. We got some strange looks from passing cyclists and horse riders, and a rude comment from a farmer passing by on his tractor. We attempted to stuff the feathers into an old feed bag, but it seemed that less than half of them found their target, and the yard ended up littered with white feathers.

The next job was to gut the birds. This was not a pleasant task. There is a fine art to removing the innards without getting the contents of the gall bladder all over the place, which would ruin the meat. Luckily Rosemarie was really skilled in this undertaking.

The meat was wonderful. Despite the birds being quite fat, all the fat drained off in the cooking, leaving the dark meat lean and tasty. And the fat was not wasted either, being ideal for Rosemarie's cake making.

6 Cattle

Our first cattle were two, small, week-old heifer calves. As we had no transport for cattle, and were not sure what to look for when buying a calf anyway, we decided to ask a dealer to get us a couple of calves of a traditional breed. I guess we were taking quite a risk as we didn't know the dealer nor what we would end up with. Quite by coincidence the calves arrived on my birthday.

The dealer arrived with his massive transporter, which he reversed with some difficulty into our yard. Once inside the yard we shut the gate just in case the calves should try to escape. He opened up the back of his lorry, and there in the vast space were these two small, rather timid, calves. They were too scared to leave the lorry and so we manhandled them one at a time into the stable we had already prepared for them. They seemed a little bemused, and looked around their new home nervously. The dealer had bought them at market the day before and told us they were about a week old.

The poor little things had been taken away from their mothers, driven to market, to the dealer's home, and then to us, all in the space of a couple of days. It was little wonder they were nervous. We felt so sorry for them, although they were too nervous to let us comfort them. We were very pleased with our purchase and couldn't have hoped for a better choice.

The larger of the two was a Hereford cross, to whom we gave the name Fudgie, and the other was an Aberdeen Angus cross, who we called Angie.

The dealer told us the calves were drinking from the bucket, which supposedly should have made life a lot easier than feeding them from a bottle. If the lambs and goat kids could be rough at feeding time, what would a calf be like?

Everything went well for a couple of days until Angie got the scours. We consulted our vet book and discovered it was very much more serious than scours in lambs, with which we were by now quite expert in dealing. It could kill within days. We didn't delay in calling the vet. It was a sign of the seriousness that he came out straight away. He prescribed a rehydration solution to counter the dehydrating effect of scours, and antibiotics. Angie seemed to pick up on the rehydration solution, but the antibiotics appeared to put her off drinking. It seemed like a vicious circle. Overall she was getting worse. We were at our wits end. We had to call the vet out on three occasions, and each time they just prescribed more antibiotics – even though that was what seemed to be causing the problem. It didn't help that we had a different vet each time, each of whom appeared to have little experience with cattle. And still poor Angie was getting no better.

We thought we were going to lose her. It was both sad and frustrating. Out of desperation, I gave her a probiotic, something we had seen advertised by a company specialising in natural remedies, and I had bought some 'just in case' a few months earlier. A probiotic is a natural preparation containing beneficial bacteria. Rather than killing off all the bacteria in the stomach as antibiotics do, probiotics add bacteria that are beneficial to the digestion. We had nothing to lose.

Not long after giving her the probiotic, while we were feeding Fudgie we offered Angie some goats' milk from a bottle. She took the proffered bottle and drank it down greedily. We could hardly believe it. Oh what a relief! We gave her as much milk as she would drink and kept our fingers crossed. The scours didn't reappear. Each day Angie was improving. Slowly she started to recover, although she would never make up for the loss of condition at such a crucial age.

Then, just as we had got over one problem, Fudgie got bloat. Again, this is more serious in cattle than bloat in goats. The veterinary practice was some seven miles away, and in the time it would take the vet to get to us Fudgie could have died. Rosemarie administered some first aid in the form of cooking oil, which had helped in the past when Lin had bloat. When the vet arrived, he congratulated Rosemarie on her quick thinking and said she had probably saved Fudgie's life. He then proceeded to use a scalpel blade to pierce the stomach, and inserted a trochar and canula to allow the gasses to escape. He left the tools with us in case we should need them again. It looked a rather horrific process, luckily one we didn't have to repeat.

The calves had to spend most of their first year inside, in their stable. When we looked out of the kitchen window, we would often see Fudgie's face trying to peer over the stable door. As she grew, more of her head was visible, until she was just about able to see us when we waved to her. Poor Angie was that much shorter and was never quite able to see over the top of the door. I even put a log in the stable near the door for them to stand on so they would be able to see out better. It wasn't long before Fudgie realised its use, and she started climbed up onto it to peer over the door. But Angie never cottoned on, or she couldn't be bothered. Or perhaps she just wasn't as nosey as Fudgie!

Based on her previous experience with young calves Rosemarie was concerned that when we let Fudgie and Angie out into the paddock for the summer they would run amok. She didn't think we'd be able to give them free rein of the paddock in case they chased the sheep. A couple of the ewes were still to lamb, and another, Helga, had a dicky ticker. I had bought a number of fencing panels, which allowed us to fence off a small area of the paddock for the calves, and we could move it and extend it once they got used to being outside. Hence it was with some trepidation we first led them, one at a time, into the small area we had fenced off for them. They seemed to be really pleased to be out, delighted to have some grass to chew on, and much to our surprise were very well behaved. Perhaps there had been nothing to worry about after all.

It worked well for a couple of weeks until one day when they appeared to be a little disturbed. Angie started to run round inside the enclosure gathering steam, and then she eventually took off and jumped over the fence into the paddock. It wasn't a clean jump and she pulled down one of the panels, bending both it and its neighbour. Fudgie looked apprehensively at the fallen fence, and longingly at the paddock. She seemed to be considering the position carefully before making her move. Eventually she walked gingerly, rather than jumped, over the limp fencing panel into the paddock.

All the while the sheep watched the proceedings with apprehension. Once in the paddock, however, Fudgie and Angie were as good as gold. They took no notice of the sheep, apparently being more interested in the new pasture than those strange woolly creatures.

We had intended to fatten both the calves, selling one on for further fattening or killing, and having the other one killed for ourselves, with some meat to sell to friends and family. But we became very attached to Fudgie with her affectionate nature, and her red/brown coat, white face, socks and undercarriage, and so we decided to keep her as a house cow. We were fond of them both, but Angie was never as forward or friendly as Fudgie.

Taking Angie to the butcher was one thing we had been dreading. Firstly there was the emotional attachment. It is easy to write with apparent detachment about having the animals butchered, but we always felt a sense of betrayal when we took one of our animals to the butcher. But at least we knew our animals had a good life and were well cared for.

Then there were the practical arrangements. I had repaired the trailer floor and had the means of transport, but I was dreading the seven-mile trip to the butcher. There were a number of awkward turns to navigate at the other end, and I was no expert at reversing the trailer.

We had been wondering how we would be able to separate Angie and Fudgie. And how we were going to get Angie into the box. We would have to coax her as, given her size, we would never be able to manhandle her if she decided to be obstinate. For several weeks Rosemarie got Angie used to the box by feeding her in there. Although not without the odd mishap or two, it was a great success, and Fudgie hadn't noticed she had been eating alone. With her head in the manger would never even notice the end of the world.

We had her booked in at the butchers for the last Monday of November, our last chance before Christmas. Rosemarie phoned to confirm the booking.

'Oh, I'm glad you called,' said the boss. 'We've been trying to phone you but you're not in the book. One of my men has gone sick. We can't do you now till after Christmas.'

'You're joking!' replied Rosemarie. 'You've already postponed us once. We wanted the beef for Christmas.'

'Sorry, love, call us back in January.'

Why did it always seem like they were doing us a favour? Having psyched ourselves up it was a great blow. Apart from anything else it meant we would have to rethink our plans for Fudgie. We had been waiting till Angie had gone before bringing Fudgie into the stable for winter, but now they would both have to come in.

We finally managed to take Angie to the butcher towards the end of January. And so we had several more weeks of worrying, imagining all the things that might go wrong. Not being able to get her into the box. Having a puncture on the trailer – for which we didn't have a spare. Or having her run off out of the yard when we got to the other end. For Rosemarie especially, a master of worrying, it was an ideal opportunity for a fertile mind to run away with itself.

In the event it all passed without a hitch, save that Fudgie started to try and climb out of the stable once we had got Angie safely in the box. She was quite a sight with her front legs hanging out over the lower stable door, as if to say, 'Wait for me Ange.' Although it had its funny side, it was really rather sad, and she could have severely injured herself if she had clambered out any further before we were able to get the top door closed.

Angie didn't seem to mind the journey at all, and was not at all stressed when we got to our destination, as we had feared. She had eaten all the beef nuts and hay we had put into the trailer for her, so she couldn't have been too put out by the journey. But it was very upsetting for us to leave her in the pen at the butchers awaiting her fate, and we kept wondering throughout the day whether she had been 'done' yet.

Poor old Fudgie was pretty upset, too, when we got home. She had never been alone and shut up before, and she must have wondered where her companion had gone. We had to keep the top stable door closed for several days whilst she calmed down. Poor thing, we felt sorry for her being alone. But after about a week she seemed quite used to the idea, so long as we regularly made a fuss of her.

As near as we could guess there was about three hundred pounds of meat from Angie. We had quite a job bagging up and freezing it all. The butcher had jointed and labelled it all, but we still spent nearly all day Saturday sorting it out and putting it into the freezers. We couldn't freeze it all in one day anyway as the freezers didn't have the capacity. We had even had to purchase a new, extra large, freezer to cater for all the extra meat, but even so it could only freeze the meat in small batches. And so Rosemarie spent a good part of Sunday, too, packing it up and sorting out batches for friends and relatives.

The money we got for the meat we sold more than paid for the butchering, but it didn't cover all the feeding costs. Our meat always seemed to be a bit fatty when compared with that in the supermarket, but it was of a far better quality and had more flavour.

Our next job was to get Fudgie in the family way. This was going to mean using artificial insemination. And in order for us to use the AI service we had to become members of the Milk Marketing Board, not that we had any intention of producing milk for sale. It all seemed a bit of a palaver just for one 'house' cow.

Catching them in season when there were the two of them was not very difficult as they would always play 'mummies and daddies' with each other. Whether or not it would be as easy when we only had Fudgie we would just have to wait and see.

As it was, Fudgie was easy to catch in season, particularly as she started to call out for a bull. Fat chance, Fudgie! We called out the AI man that afternoon for him to arrive the following morning. We had already chosen a Hereford bull which was to sire her offspring from a catalogue; it seemed a bit like computer dating by proxy.

After her breakfast Fudgie was happy enough to stay in the stable until the AI man arrived, but she was not quite so keen on being tied up, nor of having a bit of plastic tubing inserted up her unmentionables. But, thankfully, she was well behaved, and was very soon back out in the paddock as if nothing had happened.

116

To our relief she had taken first time, so we didn't have the expense or trouble of repeating the performance the following month. It was a bit of luck for beginners. Fudgie calved early one morning in her stable, a little over nine months later, in February 1992. It all happened shortly before I was due to go off to work, and Rosemarie had been up early ready to act as midwife. Not that Fudgie needed any help or encouragement. It was almost an anticlimax. But the proud 'dad' had a Polaroid snap of our new arrival to take to work to show my colleagues.

Although just after the birth Fudgie looked rather surprised at what had emerged from her rear end, she very soon set to, cleaning up her tiny calf, and she looked very proud of herself. She made a wonderful mum and seemed to take it all in her stride. We named the calf Chumpie.

Weaning Chumpie was another traumatic experience for all concerned. We had to separate the two of them, putting Fudgie and Chumpie into separate stables. As anticipated Chumpie was none too chuffed at the idea. She spent a lot of time bawling for her mum, and Fudgie would often answer back, which only made Chumpie call all the more. We shut the top stable doors for much of the time partly to keep down the noise, but also so they didn't realise the other was quite so close. However, as time went on they got used to the separation, and the following spring it was safe to let them out into the paddock together.

We had two further calves from Fudgie the following two years – Wellie, a diminutive for Wellington, and Ollie, or Olive.

And there were no real events save for an incident just before Wellie was born. We still had Chumpie, and had left her out in the paddock together with Fudgie most of the time. Fudgie's udders were quite large, showing she was only a day or so away from calving. At the time in question the two of them were in the Tringle. It was obvious as she walked around licking her lips that Chumpie was remembering how nice it was to have some of mummy's milk. You could almost see her thinking.

'We ought to separate them,' Rosemarie announced as we stood watching them.

'Oh, they'll be all right,' replied one who preferred to let things be.

Eventually Chumpie decided to make a beeline for the milky bar. All hell broke loose.

Now we had little option but to intervene. We dashed into the Tringle with the intention of getting them apart – how we proposed to do it we had no ideas, but we didn't want this great baby drinking the new, as yet unborn, calf's colostrum. Fudgie was of the same persuasion, and was trying to get away from Chumpie. Somehow or another we managed to get them apart and to get first Fudgie and then Chumpie into separate stables. Chumpie, though, had a broad grin and a white moustache! It was obviously going to be some while before they could be in the same enclosure together again.

Another little problem was when Ollie was born. It was some hours before we could get her to suckle. She didn't seem to grasp the idea at all. Knowing how important that first feed is, full of mum's colostrum, we began to get concerned. Even Fudgie seemed a bit disconcerted. It was several hours after her birth, having got them both into a stable, that we managed to attach Ollie's mouth to an udder and encourage her to suck. Even after that Ollie needed encouragement to suckle for several further days, as though, somehow, it was all too much work. Luckily Ollie suffered no long-term problems as a result of her early laziness, and she grew to be a loving, cuddly cow.

The farmland adjoining our back field was transformed into a golf course not long after it had been sold. It took a few years to set out the ground, and for the grass to grow and become established. But it wasn't long before we started to find golf balls in our field. Whether or not they were a hazzard to the animals we were not sure. We had heard scare stories about animals eating golf balls, but whether they were true or not we didn't know. The balls were certainly a nuisance. We had originally objected to the building of the course but had become resigned to its existence. There was an uneasy truce between us and the owner, a local demolition contractor, Mr Finch. One evening as dusk came on Rosemarie came rushing in.

'Come quick! Ollie's on the golf course,' she called. 'Oh, God. How are we going to get her back?'

'By keeping calm, for one thing,' I suggested, grabbing my coat and wellies.

'We'll have old Finchy suing us for compensation.'

'Let's just think about getting Ollie back for the moment shall we?'

Rosemarie had a horse on loan at the time, and she had put him out in the back field with the sheep, the goats and Ollie. Quite what happened we didn't know, but it seemed that Black Jack had wanted to get to know Ollie a little better, but she had other ideas. In running away from the horse she had run right into –

or over – the electric fence, leaving it badly sagging. She'd got into the copse, and then onto the golf course.

'You'd better take BJ in and turn off the electric fence,' I suggested. 'I'll go and see to Ollie.'

I took a bucket of Ollie's favourite beef nuts out onto the golf course. Thankfully she hadn't gone far, keeping very close to the fence. But on the wrong side! She clearly wanted to come back but dared not. She was very nervous, but after a lot of encouragement she eventually came over to me and sniffed at the bucket. Rosemarie then came out.

'Get her to come to the bucket,' said Rosemarie, having returned, 'and I'll put the halter round her neck. I'll lead her back through the gate into the copse.'

'You'll have to be careful, she's very frightened.'

After half an hour we were both getting rather frustrated. Ollie would come close to the us but not close enough to catch her.

'I think we need to leave it for a while,' I suggested. 'We and Ollie all need time to calm down.'

We finished off seeing to the rest of the animals, and then went indoors and had our tea and watched some television before going out to see to Ollie again. By the time we went back it was quite dark and we needed a torch. Ollie was still standing close to the fence, looking longingly into our field.

Several times we managed to coax her into the copse, but each time she seemed to get cold feet and went back onto the golf course again. Eventually, though, Rosemarie did manage to get the halter round her neck and we led her back into her stable for the night.

We were exhausted. We didn't dare look at all the cloven footprints on the golf course, although I had noticed one or two on the green itself. All week we half expected an irate phone call or visit, or a solicitor's letter from Mr Finch, but nothing came. He certainly could not have failed to notice he'd had an unexpected visitor of a terrestrial kind.

7 Bees

If the cattle were the largest of our livestock, then the bees were certainly the smallest – in size if not in number. Not, I suppose, that you could really call bees livestock. They are certainly not domesticated. Indeed, perhaps one of the most interesting aspects of keeping bees is that they are their own masters.

They might be interesting on an intellectual level, but you can't cuddle a bee. And you never get to know them individually the way you do with goats, sheep or cows, or even with geese.

The bees were really Rosemarie's province. Well, there wasn't much point in kitting ourselves out with two sets of protective clothing, was there? And I did my bit in consuming some of the honey, after all!

Our first hive of bees came from a dear old chap who was having to give up his bees because of his age. Mr Martin, his name was, and he had been keeping bees since he was a teenager. He clearly loved his bees and was obviously sad at having to give it all up after so many years.

There seems to be a superstition among some beekeepers that it is bad luck to exchange hard currency for bees, but Mr Martin was not one of them. We collected the hive from an allotment where he kept all his bee equipment. The allotment was full of bits of beehives, the odd hen house, a bicycle, some tools, and more bee bits and pieces.

John, of cider-drinking fame, introduced Rosemarie to the local beekeepers' association – or BKA – which she decided to join. We were surprised to learn that we should expect a visit from the bee inspector. Each locality has its own inspector, whose job is to check hives for 'foul brood', a highly infectious disease, thankfully not very common, but essential to catch at as early a stage as possible. Any colony found with the disease has to be destroyed.

We read of one beekeeper who moved to a new locality. His local beekeeping club gave him the address of the club in his new area, and he duly contacted them when he arrived. But instead of a welcome from club members, he received a visit from the bee inspector!

Our BKA was friendly enough, although they were a very individualistic bunch. They all seemed to have a different method of managing their bees, and all assumed their's was the right way.

We placed the hive by the side of the vegetable garden so the bees would have easy access to the apple trees and whatever flowers and vegetables were around. It was not a very clever place, because it meant the vegetable garden and orchard were in the direct flight path of the bees. When the bees were about we would be unable to work in either for fear of being stung.

That winter we moved the hive to a more sensible position on the other side of the orchard. There seems to be a rule of thumb in beekeeping that a hive should be moved either three feet or three miles. More than about three feet and the bees return to where their hive used to be and get lost; at three miles or so they know they're somewhere new and do not attempt to return. That's the theory. We took a gamble by moving it about thirty yards. We were lucky. It paid off. Although a handful of bees went missing, we didn't lose too many.

When a hive becomes overcrowded or the queen is getting old the bees will often swarm. It can be a handy way to get a new colony, to catch a swarm and hive it. There is usually warning of a pending swarm with a lot of activity around the hive. The old queen and about a third to a half of the bees form into a single mass of bees, and attach themselves to a tree or similar object.

In the first year we managed to increase the number of hives we had simply by placing a new empty hive beside the old one. The departing swarm simply took vacant possession of the spare hive. We had doubled the size of our apiary at a stroke. But it doesn't often work that way.

Later in the month, Lisa, a friend of Rosemarie's who also kept bees, had a swarm. Lisa had a very laid-back attitude to her bees, and tended to leave them more or less to their own devices. She couldn't be bothered with the swarm and asked Rosemarie if she wanted it. A silly question, really. Of course she did! Between them they caught the swarm in a box, and Rosemarie brought it home and hived it. This one didn't escape either, and it proved to be a very productive hive.

The following year the bees started to swarm very early – on May Day. Rosemarie enlisted the help of Lisa, and between them they managed to catch the swarm and get it into a cardboard box. It was intended to leave it until dark and then put it into a new hive.

The bees, however, had other ideas. Later that day, we found the swarm hanging on another tree. It's an awe-inspiring sight, a cluster of bees all clinging together literally hanging from the branch of a tree. But it was disconcerting to see they didn't like the box we had found for them. This time Rosemarie caught and boxed the swarm by herself. It seemed to stay that time, and after sundown she managed to hive it.

'I don't think those bees like you,' I called to Rosemarie the following morning.

'What do you mean?' she replied indignantly, coming over to the window.

I pointed out towards the orchard, and she was just in time to see the swarm taking off over the stable roof and heading off in the direction of the village. Again, it was a fascinating sight, a mass of bees flying as one. After all the effort, though, it was disappointing to see they didn't want to stay – but you don't argue with a swarm of twenty to thirty thousand bees.

Rosemarie bought some more hives and accessories from Mr Martin when he sold off the remaining items from his collection the following year. She was well pleased with her purchase and got sufficient parts for four more hives – all for the princely sum of £10.

Extracting the honey was always an exciting time. Exciting, but rather time consuming, and a very messy process. It involved removing the frames from the hives, uncapping them – that is, taking off the wax covering from the hexagonal cells of honey – and putting them into an extractor, four at a time. The job then was to whiz them round quickly to remove the honey by centrifugal force. After it had been extracted, the honey was then strained through an old pair of tights into a tub or jars.

We generally got two extractions a year. The first, mainly rape honey, was taken off in June. The second, referred to as main crop honey, was usually taken off in September.

A really good hive can produce as much as a hundred pounds of honey a year – or so we were told. But such hives are very much the exception. It is more usual to get half that amount, or less. Our hives usually produced about twenty-five pounds each, which, though pretty unimpressive, was more than we needed.

The bees need to eat during the winter, and so having taken away their winter stores, we would need to feed them. The usual feed is refined white granulated sugar made up into a syrup; other types of sugar are not pure enough. One year we bought half a twenty-five kilogram sack of sugar through the beekeepers' association, but, because of some quirk of EU rulings, it was not much cheaper than buying it in one kilo packets from the supermarket. So in subsequent years that is just what we did.

Another product of bees is beeswax. Indeed in some parts of the world it is considered to be the only product of bees. The wax comes from the cappings of the little cells which are removed when extracting the honey. There is only about a pound of beeswax for every hundred pounds of honey, so we would not have got much from our hives. It would simply not have been worth getting all the equipment to extract the wax ourselves, so we started to give the cappings to our friend John in the village. He used a solar extractor to melt the wax, which he then made up into candles. That is until I discovered how to make mead!

Ah, mead! Nectar of the gods! It is probably the easiest of all wines to make, and is apparently one of the oldest fermented drinks in Europe. It is made by adding 4lbs of honey to a gallon of water, bringing to the boil and allowing to cool. Bung in a little yeast and allow to ferment for a year or so, and that's just about it. After syphoning off the clear liquid it's ready for drinking. Although it does improve with keeping...

8 Produce

From soon after we moved in we had some of our own produce. We started off with our own goats' milk, and eggs, and, of course, the apples. From the milk Rosemarie started to make yogurt and cottage cheese, and as she was a good and keen cook, we had many other items made at least partly from our own produce. The cottage cheese was a great success, but the yogurt, though pleasant enough, was rather runny without the added gelatine of most commercial goats' milk yogurts. And, in order to have flavoured yogurts, we had to buy tins of fruit to put into the yogurt, so it was only partly homemade after all.

I attempted to make a hard cheese from the goats' milk on one occasion, but it wasn't a great success. It was rather too hard – probably as a result of my using too many weights on the cheese press – and it tasted a little like I imagine soap might taste. It wasn't a bad first attempt, really, but since it took a gallon of milk to make about a pound of cheese it was not something we felt like trying again.

It was several months before we had our own meat, initially in the form of goat and lamb, and later chicken, duck, goose, and eventually beef. We were also occasionally presented with a pheasant or partridge by a neighbour who had been given one but didn't fancy the job of plucking and gutting the bird. I can't say I blamed them, it was a lot of work just for one or maybe two meals. But if it was free we didn't like to say 'no'!

Then there was honey, ice cream, cider, apple juice and a variety of wines – some from our own fruit, but also blackberry, sloe, and crab apple from the hedgerow. And one year I made wheat wine, the wheat for which was gleaned from the field for us by our neighbour Maud.

The vegetable plot was a mixed success. We certainly had a wonderful selection of soft fruit and vegetables over the years, but it took a lot of work, and was probably not in the least cost-effective. There was very little we didn't try at one time or another.

What with the droughts, the weeds and the rabbits, moles, and birds it was a lot of work for comparatively little return. But it was always pleasing to have something we had grown on the dinner table, especially on the rare occasions we had visitors.

In the fruit line we had rhubarb, raspberries, blackcurrants, red currants, gooseberries, and one or two hybrids. The strawberry plants lasted a couple of seasons before being subsumed by the grass, nettles, and bindweed. We also had a plum tree in the paddock which gave a regular supply of fruit for very little effort. And there were always some blackberries and sloes from the hedgerow as well as our own supply of walnuts.

Potatoes were probably our most successful vegetable crop. Rosemarie had always been very fond of her potatoes, and so she always planted a good number of seed potatoes of different varieties every year. Although they were usually a success there were never enough to last us a full year.

One year Rosemarie decided to try an interesting change from potatoes. Jerusalem artichokes, not to be confused with globe artichokes. They were ready in the winter, by which time we had used up most of the potatoes we had grown. They seemed a bit like undercooked potatoes – but then maybe they were undercooked! But the really interesting part is their side effect.

Anyone who thought baked beans, Brussels sprouts or rhubarb were antisocial, should try Jerusalem artichokes! They really can make you feel quite uncomfortable. One day at work, following a meal with artichokes the previous evening, I had to sit through a two-hour meeting, tensely controlling myself. The only time I was able to get vaguely comfortable was when someone coughed or blew their nose. After that episode, 'fartichokes' were banished from weekday meals!

Our other successes included broad beans, runner beans, spinach, leeks, onions, kale greens, and garlic. Not to mention garden mushrooms, which came free! In truth, our greatest success in the vegetable plot was probably flowers, but you can't eat them! Amongst the less successful crops were carrots, peas, sweet corn and Brussels sprouts. Either the drought, the moles or rabbits got most of them.

For the first couple of years we used to pick the apples, bag them up and leave them for sale on a table by the drive. The previous owners had done so for several years, they said. Only occasionally would goods go missing without being paid for. It was very common in the eighties, before rural crime was really heard of, to find produce of all sorts being sold at the garden gate. Fruit, vegetables, cut flowers and plants. In the first year of trying this we sold more than a hundred pounds of apples that way.

The third year, I decided to make some cider instead of selling the apples. I even went to the extreme of purchasing a small fruit crusher and press to chop up the apples and then squeeze the juice out. We fed the leftover pulp to the goats, sheep and cows, who loved it. The trouble was I got rather carried away and even started collecting windfalls from neighbours and friends. And eventually sacks of apples started arriving on the doorstep unannounced. It was as if once started I was unable to stop. By the end of the season I had twenty-five gallons of cider! We also had several gallons of unfermented pure apple juice, much of which we froze. Since it took about twenty pounds of apples to make a gallon of juice, I must have pulped more than five hundred pounds of apples! Sadly, even giving away much of the cider there was still too much to drink. Not that it was wasted. Thoroughly diluted, it made an excellent liquid in which to soak the animals' sugar beet. In subsequent years we extracted the juice to drink just as pure apple juice.

When we started selling our goats' milk – not that we sold a lot, as I have already explained – there were few regulations regarding the production and sale of goats' milk. It was perhaps a little strange, given that it is often sold as being more healthy than cows' milk. It was perhaps inevitable that things would change. After a few years, regulations were introduced requiring the preparation of food for human consumption to be done in a separate room with its own equipment. And the domestic kitchen was not suitable for this. So even had we not given up anyway the regulations would have stopped us.

Eggs were one product for which we found a ready market. Once we became known, we couldn't produce enough eggs to meet the demand. Fresh free range eggs are so much nicer than those bought in the supermarket – which are often a couple of weeks old anyway – and our regular customers recognised that.

In the first few years, before the salmonella scares, we were able to sell our excess eggs without any trouble. But then more new regulations required birds to be regularly tested for salmonella, which put paid to that. Keepers with up to twenty-four birds had to have every one tested, whilst those with five hundred or more only had to have sixty birds tested. And, of course, you payed for however many birds you had tested. It simply wasn't worth the expense of having the birds tested when we had so few. Although we could eat the eggs ourselves, we were unable to sell our eggs after that. Like most of the regulations that have been introduced in recent years, they seemed to discriminate against the small producer.

One of our first money making schemes was to plant some Christmas trees. They were supposed to be fast growing and should have been saleable within a few years. We ordered a hundred, but unfortunately we left ordering them till right at the end of the season and the supplier could only find fifty decent Christmas trees, and so he made up the order with Scots Pine. What we wanted the pine trees for I can't imagine.

Rosemarie planted all the trees over a period of several days while I was at work. It was hard work in our heavy clay soil, but she finished the job. Most of them seemed to survive the cold winters and the hot, dry, summers, but because of the dry summers they took a long time in growing. Then in keeping the grass down, one or two Christmas trees also got chopped off at the knees. And then, just as they started to get to a saleable height, Rosemarie decided she didn't want to part with the 'babies' she had tended for so many years!

We were never short of sweaters. Rosemarie spun and knitted many of our own fleeces, as well as several she had bought. The sweaters were usually named after their original owners. I had a Helga, a Vashti and a Mopsy, and Rosemarie had an Em and an Eddo. We had jumpers for every occasion knitted from home spun yarn – ones for working, ones for best, one with sleeves, sleeveless ones, patterned ones, plain ones, pullovers and cardigans. The Icelandic fleeces made particularly hardwearing jumpers, and the Gotland fleeces made very soft ones.

We sold a few fleeces to other hand spinners, but Rosemarie was always careful about which ones she sold. She usually wanted to keep for herself the first shearing from any of our sheep.

'We can't sell Em's fleece,' she contended. 'And Meryl's is such an exceptional quality. And Vashti's is such an unusual colour.' And so it went on. With what she bought as well, the collection of fleeces in the stable, dining room and lounge seemed only to get larger.

'But,' as she pointed out, 'it's a cheap hobby.'

9 Trials and Tribulations

Friday 6 January 1995 is a day I shall remember vividly for the rest of my life. Fudgie, our beloved five-and-a-half-year old Hereford 'house' cow, had been acting strangely for several weeks. She was thinner than usual – though still in better condition than many commercial cows. And she had become more nervous, and had started to twitch her head.

It was my job to call out the vet, whilst Rosemarie paid yet another visit to the dentist. I was not much looking forward to it. You can't look after an animal for more than five years without noticing when something is wrong, but to explain it to a stranger is not always easy.

The vet duly arrived and confirmed our worst fears. He said he was 90 per cent sure that Fudgie had BSE or 'mad cow disease'. Any terminal illness was bad enough, but there was a stigma with BSE and it would be such an ignominious end for a fine beast. The vet was careful to say it wasn't our fault. Not that it helped much. He explained they still had much to learn about the disease, but the most likely cause was feed contaminated by protein from scrapie-infected sheep.

Why feed merchants should have put animal remains in ruminant feed is still something I cannot come to terms with. But I was even more horrified to learn that whilst this was banned in 1988, some feeds still carried the prohibited substance a year or two after that. I felt particularly bitter as we had deliberately chosen a local feed merchant, a family firm of some national repute.

Since BSE was a notifiable disease and Fudgie would have to be put down, he said he would contact the Ministry of Agriculture for us. Shortly after, I received a phone call from the MAFF, followed by a visit from the Ministry vet. We had heard how some could be rather officious so I was rather apprehensive about the visit. But it was a relief to find the young lady very sympathetic, especially when I explained the suspect beast *was* our 'herd'.

By then Rosemarie had returned and I had some moral support. The vet confirmed she suspected BSE, but explained she wanted to make a second, and possibly further visits before she could be certain and before ordering slaughter.

There was then about three-quarters of an hour of paperwork to be completed, which we conducted over a cup of tea. We had to tick off all the symptoms Fudgie had exhibited from a long list, and provide details of when was she born, where we got her from, and precisely what we fed her, together with dates! As luck would have it, Fudgie had lost her ear tag and I had never noted the number. But we still had all the feed bills for the last eight years, as well as the phone number of the dealer from whom we bought Fudgie as a calf. He would probably have a note of the ear tag number.

Although it seemed just a lot of bureaucratic paperwork, it became clear that much more information was needed in order to help the vets learn more about BSE. The original 1990 list of symptoms of the disease was just fifteen lines; the latest was over two pages! Although it didn't help us much, we were assured the disease was on the decline, so it looked as though it was not passed down from mothers to offspring.

If – or, more likely, when – the Ministry ordered slaughter, we would get financial compensation equivalent to what we would be likely to get at market. It would be good to make some money out of something, but for us to do so out of BSE just added to the insult. And it would not compensate for the emotional trauma or the loss of a friend. Another aspect of caring for an animal for several years is that you inevitably become attached to it. And we were certainly very fond of our dear old Fudgie.

Later that evening as I was just settling down in front of the open fire to watch the early evening news, I heard an urgent call from Rosemarie.

'Come outside!'

'What?'

'Just come, will you!'

Muttering under my breath, I rushed outside to find our flock of sheep – all eight of them – in the yard. Rosemarie explained she had just been putting the dogs out 'to do a poo', when she heard a squeak, which sounded rather like a dog that had just come nose-to-wire with the electric fence. She had rushed out to the back field to find all the sheep in a huddle and two large black dogs showing just a little too much interest in 'our girls'. The sheep were only too happy to follow 'mummy' back to the paddock next to the house; they needed no second invitation.

Sheep worrying had long been a concern, and as a matter of course we reported the incident to the police. They admitted there was little hope of finding the dogs or their owner. Needless to say when we went back to look, we couldn't find the dogs, and as it was dark, Rosemarie couldn't even say what breed they were. The PC informed us that, although no physical harm had come to the sheep, we would have been quite within our right to shoot the dogs. I was never sure if I'd have been able to shoot a dog if we caught one worrying our sheep, but I guess if it was a choice of our sheep or someone's dog then I'd have found an answer.

After things had calmed down, we realised how lucky we had been. A potential disaster had been averted. None of the ewes had been harmed – shaken, perhaps, but not stirred. Had Rosemarie not found them just when she did, we believed we would almost certainly have been faced with eight dead or seriously maimed sheep. The horror of it didn't bear thinking about.

Although I've not experienced sheep molesting at first hand, it is one experience I should be more than happy to forgo. I knew, though, that it caused enormous distress to both the sheep and the owner. Perhaps the most worrying aspect is the ignorance of many dog owners who believe their 'Fido' is incapable of such acts of wanton violence. One neighbour whose dog frequently used to escape, when confronted simply replied, 'Oh, he'd only lick them to death.'

But the simple truth is that any dog can turn killer. It starts innocently enough by the dog taking an interest in the sheep. As the sheep move nervously away, it becomes a game and the dog bounds after the frightened creatures. The sheep and dog run faster and faster until the whole thing becomes a dreadful massacre.

Only when we finally sat down for the evening, much later, did I think to ask Rosemarie about her tooth. Even for her it had been far from her mind for most of the day. This had been by far the most traumatic day in our eight years of the 'good life'. If another occurred this lifetime, it would be too soon. Given the date, it seemed as though Friday the thirteenth had come a week early!

But we still had a two-week wait for the Ministry vet to return...

That fortnight was one of the longest I can recall. We had to watch, helpless and hopeless, as Fudgie's condition deteriorated. Slowly, but surely. It was a miserable time – for us anyway. Fudgie, though nervous and fidgety, didn't seem to be in any real distress.

The day of reckoning eventually arrived and to our relief the vet decided she would have to put Fudgie down. She explained she would need to inject Fudgie with a sedative before administering a lethal dose of anaesthetic. We wondered how she would get close enough to give the sedative. Fudgie was averse to needles at the best of times. In the nervous state she was in with BSE it would be nigh on impossible. We voiced our opinions, but the vet knew best, young and inexperienced though we knew her to be. She wanted Rosemarie and me to hold the beast against the wall of the stable using a couple of the metal hurdles. We seemed to have little choice but to try it her way. Very carefully we managed to get Fudgie into a corner and as quiet as we could. She looked apprehensively at the vet as she produced the syringe. The vet came close, and the needle and Fudgie's rump came together.

Fudgie jumped up and shot forward, knocking the hurdles and us out of the way, and almost taking the stable door off its hinges as she tried to get over it. Rosemarie and I both stood there numb, shaking with shock and wondering what she would do next. The poor cow was clearly very agitated now. Even in her last moments she was to have no dignity. We watched as she wandered nervously round the stable. As she calmed down a little, we made quickly, but very gingerly, for the exit. How none of us was hurt, was a mystery to us all.

Somewhat subdued, the vet decided to try 'Plan B'.

She telephoned the office and called for reinforcements in the form of a colleague with a tranquilliser gun. So we were faced with more waiting, whilst we calmed ourselves down with a cup of tea. Meanwhile our poor Fudgie was making a gallant effort to calm down, too.

Gratefully, I absented myself to the office at Rosemarie's suggestion.

'Go on,' she said, 'you go up to the office and find something else to do. I can manage all right and if we need you I'll call.'

'Are you sure?' I asked, grateful for an excuse to get away.

'Yes, I can cope.'

She told me afterwards it had taken twice the normal amount of sedative to quieten Fudgie down sufficiently. And then she needed more than twice the amount of anaesthetic. It was three and a half hours before Fudgie was finally 'asleep'. Fit and well built, she was a fighter till the end. We had always felt a pride whenever someone had commented on how fit and well she had looked. When I went downstairs at lunchtime, I plucked up the courage to go and say my farewell.

As if we hadn't spent enough time waiting around, we then had to wait for the lorry to arrive to take away the carcass. It could have been anything up to twenty-four hours. Luckily, though, it was only about three. No longer the Fudgie we had cared for for the last five and a half years, her body was winched unceremoniously onto the back of the lorry.

I gave a last, pathetic, tearful wave goodbye as the lorry turned out of the drive.

Rats were a perennial challenge to us. The corners of all the stable doors had been nibbled away when we arrived, although initially we didn't appreciate their significance.

It wasn't long before we appeared to have a rat in the food store. There were holes in all the bags of animal feeds. We bought a rat trap and tried to catch it, but to no avail. Quite what we would have done had we been successful and actually caught a live rat, I have no idea. But, luckily we didn't. Next we tried to stop it getting into the stable, thinking it only went in the stable at night, but we eventually realised it was already inside. Finally I found a piece of drainpipe, blocked up one end and part filled it with rat poison – the one whose advertisements used to have a picture of a dead rat with the caption, 'Another satisfied customer'. Yes, okay, perhaps it is a bit sick, but there wasn't much room for rats on our farm.

The poison seemed to be disappearing, so I topped it up. After a few days no more poison had gone, which suggested that ratty was dead. But where was the body? We had several bales of hay on pallets in the store, so it seemed most likely he was somewhere underneath the pallets. I couldn't do anything straight away with all the hay there.

When we had finally used the last bale, several months later, Rosemarie and I went out to see what we had caught, and dispose of the body. I gingerly lifted up the pallets one by one. After a while I found my quarry.

'Hey, Rose,' I called. 'It's a biggy.'

Rosemarie was nowhere to be seen.

I carefully lifted up the rat using the longest handled fork I could find, and, with great relief, dumped it into a rubbish bag, together with its droppings and as much of the contaminated hay as I could collect up.

It was not until I had put the bag into the dustbin that Rosemarie showed her face again. 'Has it gone?' she enquired with a grimace.

Haymaking was always a stressful time of the year for us. All it needs is a week or two of decent sun without a spot of rain. Not too much to ask, even of the British weather, one might think. The time for making hay varies depending on how well the grass has grown, as well as – of course – the weather. It could be any time between about June and August.

There is nothing like the smell of new-mown hay, the sight of a shorn field and a barn filled with a few hundred bales of hay, and the warm feeling of satisfaction knowing you have enough winter feed for the animals. Or is that warm feeling more the result of the celebrations? Unfortunately we had very few opportunities for celebrating a good hay harvest. We attempted to make hay for several years until the stress of it all became too much, and having become convinced we were jinxed we decided to buy in our hay.

Our first summer we asked a contractor if the paddock would make suitable hay given the rather large amount of weeds it contained. It needed cutting anyway, but he said we should get a reasonable crop of hay from it. He then proceeded to turn up to cut the grass on a dull drizzly day after what had been a fairly wet period. It rained every day afterwards for weeks, and we ended up having to collect up all the sodden mass of grass and burn it. It was a tiring, time-consuming and depressing job, the more so as we would now have to buy in some hay. It taught me a valuable lesson, but I have often since wondered about my ignorance in allowing the contractor to cut the grass when he did. We had one minor consolation in that he never got paid for the job.

In the second year we had the back field. We decided to make hay on that, keeping the sheep and goats grazing in the paddock. There were rather a lot of 'volunteer' oats among the grass, the remnants of the previous owner's last crop. The grass (and oats) were cut at a suitable time, and David our contractor – not surprisingly we'd found ourselves a new one this year – came and turned the crop several times. It needed turning many more times than would have been necessary had it just been grass. The grass had dried out nicely, but the oats were still green even after a couple of weeks. The weather was due to break and so we felt obliged to bale it regardless. Although we got some usable hay, much of it went mouldy, and we ended up using most of it as compost.

The following year was a little better. Unfortunately there had been a hot spring with little rain, which meant the grass hadn't grown much. But we did end up with some quite passable hay. We were very much in the hands of the contractor, both for advice as to when the grass was ready to cut, and when he could fit us in with all his other work. David eventually came to cut it at the end of June.

After it was cut, we had a shower or two of rain every day for a week. Rosemarie was going spare.

'We'll never get any hay,' she moaned. 'We'll have to burn it all.'

David assured us it would be okay so long as the hay had not been turned. And in any case the odd shower wouldn't do too much harm. Rosemarie was not convinced.

After a further week we had some really dry weather, and the hay was promptly turned and baled. It was not perfect, and only two hundred bales off a four-acre field was a very poor return. But it was satisfying to have our own hay and know we had some winter feed for the animals. And, although we were not to know it at the time, it turned out to be the best hay we were ever to get.

It was hard work just taking in the bales, loading them forty at a time onto the trailer and bringing it in, unloading them, and then stacking them all. We were glad to have plenty of time in which to bring them all inside. There is nothing worse than having to rush to get a field of hay inside quickly before the rains start – except doing so while it is actually raining. Which, of course, did happen another year. And then we were out carting in bales in the drizzle till well gone midnight.

The wind was another natural feature that did not always work in our favour. Being on the edge of the 'East Anglian Prairies', the land was rather flat with few natural features or trees to break the wind – if you'll pardon the expression. We were just out of range of the hurricanes of October 1987, but then we were used to high winds in any case. We were inevitably caught napping and would find anything that had been left lying around outside being blown all over the yard. Quite often the whole house would shake in the winds, and our vivid imaginations would wonder what damage was being caused.

Apart from slates on the roof coming loose quite regularly, however, the winds caused very little damage.

The main exception was the garage I had purchased for the tractor. It was fine for the cars to stand outside in all weathers, but not the tractor. This particular garage came as a kit and was delivered by post. The poor postman seemed quite bemused that he should have had to deliver such a large, heavy, and bulky set of parcels. He was obviously pleased to be shot of it as it almost filled his little van.

I decided to erect the garage in the orchard just behind the stables. The construction consisted of aluminium struts with PVC panels. There were hundreds of nuts and bolts. And just to make it interesting there were dozens of missing parts, which I only found to be missing when I actually needed them. So assembly was very much a stop-start affair, as I found another missing part and had to wait several days for it to be delivered. But eventually the whole thing was complete and the tractor was nicely snuggled up for the winter.

However, after one of our windy nights I came down one morning to find the entire garage parked halfway up one of the Poplar trees in the back garden. It had thankfully been lifted right over the tractor, which hadn't even been touched. It was a shock at the time, and I just stood there open mouthed and transfixed, but after a few minutes I saw the funny side and had a good laugh. Rosemarie, though, was a bit bemused when she came out to find me standing at the gate to the orchard having a good chuckle.

The 'plastic garage' had obviously not been a very successful product as, when I phoned to find the current price for my insurance claim, I was informed that they had stopped making it. So I replaced it with a more sturdy, but slightly smaller, wooden shed.

❖

10 Round Up

The end of our farming experience came almost exactly ten years after it had begun. Rosemarie and I had come to realise we wanted different things from life. I suppose, had we but realised it at the time, we had stopped communicating some while ago. And, as well as the obvious anguish of parting, it was going to mean giving up the little farm we had come to love so much.

Having come to such a difficult decision, we then had the momentous task of selling all the live and deadstock, as well as our home, and each buying our own new property. We had reduced the number of animals quite drastically over the previous two or three years, but we were left with those we loved most. And we had amassed no end of tools, equipment and junk.

We decided to save ourselves two or three thousand pounds in estate agent's fees by advertising the holding privately in a horsey magazine. We were delighted at the response we received. People came to view from quite far afield, although our eventual buyer came from only a few miles away.

It was just our luck that only a week before the advert came out a crack in the kitchen wall, which had given us no cause for concern for almost ten years, should suddenly open up. It seemed the extension was trying to part company from the original house. It gave us several weeks of anxious moments wondering what to do since we were not covered for subsidence on our insurance. What was it going to cost to put right? Should we get it fixed now, in the depths of winter, or wait? Greatly to our relief the lady who eventually bought the farm had a full structural survey before making us an offer, so she knew what she was in for.

The house and farm were sold with resident cat.

I haven't mentioned the cats much. Probably because they were not a major part of our lives. Rosemarie had little time for cats, and I was allergic to them, so they lived outside in the stables. Rosemarie had been taught at her mother's knee how to say, 'psst, dirty old cat!' with great feeling. Given this state of affairs it is some wonder that we got any cats at all, but we wanted something to keep down the rat population, and that at least was our rationale. And they were free! We were given two ginger tom kittens by the proverbial friend of a friend. One was all ginger and so he was named Ginger; the other had a white patch on his chest and was called Whitey. Despite us showing them little affection they were very friendly cats, and we were genuinely saddened when Whitey was knocked down and killed by a car.

It has to be said they did little to keep down the rat population, but the cats frequently returned with mice, voles and rabbits. Of the mice and voles, all that was usually left was the innards. But we frequently used to see them dragging home a rabbit almost their own size. That was quite a sight.

It was quite surprising how, having made the decision to sell up, everything seemed to fall into place. The tractor was the first item to be sold, followed by most of the implements, the tractor shed, and various other tools and equipment.

Kady, our only goat by then, went back to her original owner, Mrs Dunhill. When she heard of our changing circumstances, Mrs D was only too delighted to have Kady home with her. By this time Mrs D was almost housebound. Her daughter came to collect Kady, and she said they were going to dry her off and keep her just as a pet. A very satisfactory solution all round, it seemed. Mrs Dunhill had her beloved goat back, and Kady could enjoy her last few years just being pampered! Kady was such a good milker, though, we wondered how easy it was going to be to keep her dry.

The sheep – we just had six by then – went to a smallholder, a friend of a friend, who already had several sheep. When we met the couple, we felt sure Gottie and the girls would have a good home, as well as some more ovine company.

That just left Ollie. Dear great lumbering beast. Despite advertising her in the local paper we had no luck selling her. Not a single enquiry. Winter was not a good time to be selling an animal anyway, when they would need to be kept inside and fed up. And the BSE crisis had severely reduced the price of cattle. We thought the only option was going be to sell her at market, whereas we really wanted to find a good home for her, too.

Reluctantly we rang Robin, another local farmer, who had previously taken some of our lambs to market for us. He would be happy to take our heifer to market, he said, but it would not be for a week or two as he would be on holiday and then would need to catch up with things on his farm. That was no problem for us. To our surprise, though, an hour or so later he rang back and asked if we would consider selling Ollie to him. He had a small herd of cattle and was looking for another breeding cow.

It couldn't be better as far as we, and no doubt Ollie, were concerned. So, much to our delight, in the end we found a happy home for Ollie with a motley crew of other cows for company, and a giant of a bull for something else.

The stables were ideal for hoarding all those things that might come in useful 'some day'. Needless to say some day never arrived, and we never found a use for most of the items we held on to. There were piles of timber, which we left for the new owner. Sixty kilograms of nuts and bolts I had 'invested' in several years earlier were split into several lots and disposed of amongst friends.

We had to throw out a couple of dozen sheep fleeces, which had been taking up a large part of one of the stables. Never being one for throwing anything away, it pained Rosemarie to do so, but she would never spin them all now, and several of them had started to disintegrate anyway.

We had a bonfire for many of the things we had kept for anything up to ten years, including a chest of drawers with woodworm! And there were many other things that in reality we would never have found a use for. More than a hundred paper feed sacks went to the recycling centre, and a dozen or more wine-making demijohns were despatched to the charity shop. And that was just the tip of the iceberg.

Even the freezers hadn't escaped our hoarding. There were dozens of pounds of beef still in both freezers, so there seemed little choice about what to have for the Sunday roast for the foreseeable future. And as we dug down we found many frozen meals and bag upon bag of cooked fruit. How long some of this had been there we didn't like to contemplate too closely.

Our little farm seemed so quiet and empty without the animals. It was quite eerie. And quiet. And sad. The paddock, back field and stables were all empty. And it was strange not having to get up early to feed and tend to any of them, save for feeding and walking the dogs.

A farming life of self-sufficiency in the company of animals, with the bustle of the city all but a dim and distant memory, may be many people's idea of a rural idyll. For most, though, it remains just a dream. And perhaps that is just as well. Dreams are, perhaps, sometimes better remaining no more than just dreams.

But for those who take the plunge it is not long before real life occurs in the form of pests and diseases, the weather, death, economic realities, legislation, and human incompetence. A recognition that perhaps, after all, things are not always as easy as they seem.

Most people who have not tried farming, whether they're townies or not, seem to imagine the life of a farmer to be a very simple existence. And a very rewarding one. Whilst our experiences on seven and a half acres hardly compares with running a large commercial farm, there are some similarities. Except for a grant for the hedge and compensation for having our Fudgie destroyed when she had BSE, we never received any of the subsidies the layman associates with farming. Not that we expected any. And, of course, we never had any economies of scale. However, whatever size, we all had to contend with Mother Nature and bureaucracy.

I have often wondered why we didn't give up earlier with some of the things that didn't go the way we planned. One reason, certainly, was my stubbornness. Rosemarie, I often felt, seemed often prepared to give up at the first hurdle. But I always wanted to keep trying, often beyond the point where any reasonable person would have given up. No doubt these opposing attitudes led to some of our difficulties. Another reason is, I now believe, that I had somehow set a time span for this episode of my life. Soon after we moved in I told Rosemarie I expected us to be there for at least ten years. Call it a wish fulfilment or a premonition, perhaps, but it seems as though that one statement set the boundary for our farming experience.

I didn't appreciate it at the time, but our farming experience was a very formative part of my spiritual journey through life. Although I had attended church, both as a boy and later as an adult, I had never really thought about anything spiritual. In fact it has taken several re-readings – and re-workings – of this book to come to realise just what this life experience has meant to me.

I was made redundant after a couple of years on the farm, when the firm I worked for was taken over. After the initial shock of finding I was surplus to requirements, I began to realise this was the opportunity I needed. All my working life I had said I wanted to be my own boss. But I always lacked the courage to leave a well paid job and branch out on my own. Finally, it seemed, the Universe had supported me in my desire, by giving me the necessary boot up the backside. It was as though, having spoken of being my own boss for long enough, it was inevitable that it would come about eventually.

Almost without realising it I had mentioned my desire to be my own boss to many colleagues, some of whom had since moved on to other jobs. So it was hardly surprising that I soon found someone who wanted to take me on a six-month contract. I was now a self-employed 'consultant'.

What a difference that made. No longer did I have to do what the boss wanted. Gulp, I was the boss! But then I soon found there was no one else to make all the decisions. I had to do that myself. There was no one to lean on. No one else to blame. Perhaps for the first time in my life I was beginning to learn to trust myself. And it wasn't always easy. It was up to me to decide under what terms I would do business. Set my own charge rates, go out and meet new clients, write the proposals, do the work, and chase the bills. I had excitement and nervousness all in one package. And as I found out, working for myself was not without its own stresses and uncertainties, but at least I was becoming the author of my own destiny on the work front.

One of the biggest discoveries for me during those ten years was the realisation that negative thinking could create an adverse result. How many times did we need to have a poor hay harvest, whilst everyone else around had a successful crop, or for our sheep to be the only flock for miles around to get maggots, for me to realise that?

But it was a far cry from the realisation that if pessimistic thoughts could create an unfavourable result, then perhaps optimistic thinking could create a favourable outcome.

I came to realise how much more prevalent sceptical thinking is than constructive thoughts. In our lives, certainly, but also perhaps in the world at large. It was something Rosemarie and I both recognised in each other – and were only too willing to point out – but, funnily enough, we never recognised it in ourselves. How often when asked what we wanted would we respond with what we didn't want? Or when asked what was working, did we start by explaining what was not working. How often did we sabotage our efforts by saying, 'Oh that will never work!' or, 'You can't do that!' Surprise, surprise. When we started with this premise, seldom did it work! And lo and behold when we tried, we couldn't do that! It is little surprise, really, because by starting off with the assumption that we would fail, we were not open to the possibility of success.

And how often would we worry about something that might or might not happen? What a waste of energy worrying is in the first place, without dwelling on what may never occur anyway.

It was not as if there were insufficient examples of when a positive approach had achieved a successful outcome. After all, how many times had I managed to pen the sheep, or complete some construction or other despite a certain significant other person's scepticism? And then it seems so much easier to put such successes down to fluke or good luck than to credit ourselves with good judgement or a job well done.

And there was the time Cindy had been badly bitten by another dog. It was very distressing. The wound was most severe, and the vet and Rosemarie had serious doubts it would heal at all. Rosemarie went away to Devon for a week, and I took the opportunity to ignore the vet's prescription, preferring to use a couple of herbal remedies. The wound was getting noticeably better each day with this treatment, and by the time Rosemarie returned it had almost healed. Neither she nor the vet could believe their eyes. They thought it was nothing short of a miracle. But, with my lack of medical training, I was blissfully unaware of the possible difficulties, and Cindy and I never doubted she would get better. And get better she did.

However, although I recognised a link between thoughts and results, just how thoughts could create a physical manifestation was quite another matter. This was something I was unable to get to grips with for some while.

Perhaps it was all this that first helped me appreciate that there is more to life than simply what we can see, hear, taste, smell, and touch. Although I would probably have recoiled from calling it that at the time, I guess it is what I now consider the spiritual side of life. And having discovered a spiritual dimension to my life, I was keen to discover more. Perhaps there are those reading who feel uncomfortable relating everyday activities to the profound. Well, okay. That's fine! I am not suggesting my views are right, I'm merely sharing my philosophy of life. If you happen to agree, that's great; and if it gives you something with which disagree, then that's great, too.

Living so close to nature as we were, it is difficult to ignore many of the more obvious connections with

'Mother Nature'. The open space, the weather, peace and quiet, the soil, almost daily life-and-death situations, and home-grown vegetables, to name but a few. But to leave it there would, I think, be to miss the point.

For me, the spiritual is not to do with religion. I would not wish to get into a theological debate here, much as I might enjoy it. But how many wars have been started through a lack of tolerance of religious differences? Spirituality is not about separating parts of ourselves or our lives, into the secular and the sacred. Rather it is about acknowledging that everything we do, feel, and think, has a spiritual element to it. And whether we choose to accept or ignore it, the spiritual side is still there.

How good we are at recognising differences in other people, rather than looking for things we have in common. Life isn't, or shouldn't be, about us and them. We're all in this 'life' thing together, and the idea that for one person to win another has to lose doesn't seem to make a lot of sense. That kind of thinking only starts wars, it never stops or prevents them. Why shouldn't we be able to create a situation in which everyone gets to win.

And how easy it is to recognise patterns of behaviour in other people, but not in ourselves! It didn't take me long to recognise that the things Rosemarie found irritating in me were things she did herself. But it never occurred to me that the reverse might also be true! I can now see the truth in the old childhood retort that, 'It takes one to know one.'

The process of turning out and throwing away our possessions of several years was quite a traumatic one. Whilst it was satisfying to fill the dustbin with unwanted things, it sometimes brought back memories, some good and some not so good. And some items were particularly difficult to chuck out, until I realised that it did not invalidate those memories or experiences. Whatever happened to the possessions those memories and experiences would still be there, part of my past. It seems to me in retrospect that turning out is a cleansing experience. It enables us to get rid of the old, and make room for something new to take its place. So often there is so much clutter in our lives and our homes that there's no room for something new. And there is always something new for all of us.

Another lesson I learned was the need for forgiveness. If we harbour a grudge against someone, whether the cause of that grudge is real or imagined, it doesn't resolve anything. The subject of our grievance is seldom aware of or affected by it. All it does is to keep the wound open. And it is only us that suffers. By forgiving and forgetting we are able to move on to something new, and not live in the past. It doesn't mean we have to condone the act, but just give up the resentment.

To have spent ten years living the 'good life' was both a wonderful experience and a great privilege for me. Despite the setbacks and difficulties we encountered, there were plenty of successes. Every new life we helped create, every bowl of fruit or vegetables, and every pint of goats' milk was no doubt a success. And whatever happened it is a period of my life about which I have no regrets. Each success was a great joy and every setback a chance to learn and grow.

To share the joys and pains of life of some of the animal friends with whom we share this little planet is a gift beyond measure. I defy anyone who has kept animals to deny they have something to teach us. Each animal – and, despite my reservations, I guess I would still include chickens – has its own personality and, I am convinced, its own spirit. To serve our animal friends, I believe now, was my purpose in life during those ten years. The loss of poor dear Fudgie with BSE still haunts me whenever I think of her, but it also helps me understand something about how man has exploited and let down the animal kingdom.

With all the furore over CJD – the human equivalent of BSE – we did wonder, briefly, whether we would get the disease. After all, we had given Angie the same feeds as Fudgie, and we had eaten parts of two of Fudgie's offspring. But what would be the point of worrying about it now? If we caught the disease, we caught it, worrying couldn't change anything.

However, this and my regard for animals did make me question whether I should become a vegetarian. There doesn't seem to be a lot to be said for not eating meat on humanitarian grounds but continuing to consume dairy products. After all, in order to give milk a cow must have a calf every year. And what is to happen to all those calves? As yet I don't have an answer. Or am I just pretending not to know? In any case it is up to every individual to make up their own minds. Far be it for me to prescribe what others should or should not do – any more than I expect others to tell me I'm wrong!

It was a great wrench to sell up and leave the farm, and it seemed like the end of a dream. Indeed that's just what it was. On top of all the upheaval, moving back to the big City was going to be quite a challenge, too. Perhaps one day I shall move back to the country.

Who knows where I will feel led to next? But the end of one episode is the beginning of another. And as one door closes so another opens – here's hoping the corridor between is not too long!